8/24
£1.

CityPack
Istanbul

CHRISTOPHER AND MELANIE RICE

Christopher and Melanie Rice have travelled extensively in Europe and the Near East and enjoy sharing their experiences with others. Over the last 20 years they have written numerous guidebooks and travel articles.

City-centre map continues on inside back cover

AA Publishing

Contents

life **5 – 12**

how to organise your time **13 – 22**

top 25 sights **23 – 48**

Index...94–95

About this book...4

About this book

KEY TO SYMBOLS

✚	map reference on the fold-out map accompanying this book (see below)
✉	address
☎	telephone number
🕐	opening times
🍴	restaurant or café on premises or near by
Ⓜ	nearest underground train station
🚇	nearest overground train station
🚌	nearest bus route
⛴	nearest riverboat or ferry stop
♿	facilities for visitors with disabilities
✋	admission charge
↔	other nearby places of interest
❓	tours, lectures, or special events
➤	indicates the page where you will find a fuller description
ℹ	tourist information

CityPack Istanbul is divided into six sections to cover the six most important aspects of your visit to Istanbul. It includes:

- The authors' views of the city and its people
- Itineraries, walks and excursions
- The top 25 sights to visit – as selected by the authors
- Features about different aspects of the city that make it special
- Detailed listings of restaurants, hotels, shops and nightlife
- Practical information

In addition, easy-to-read side panels give fascinating extra facts and snippets, highlights of places to visit and invaluable practical advice.

CROSS-REFERENCES

To help you make the most of your visit, cross-references, indicated by ➤, show you where to find additional information about a place or subject.

MAPS

- **The fold-out map** in the wallet at the back of the book is a comprehensive street plan of Istanbul. All the map references given in the book refer to this map. For example, the Süleymaniye Camii on Süleymaniye Caddesi has the following information: ✚ K11 – indicating the grid square of the map in which the Süleymaniye Camii will be found.
- **The city-centre map** found on the inside front and back covers of the book itself are for quick reference. They show the Top 25 Sights in the city, described on pages 24–48, which are clearly plotted by number (❶ – ㉕, not page number) from west to east.

PRICES

Where appropriate, an indication of the cost of an establishment is given by £ signs: **£££** denotes higher prices, **££** denotes average prices, while **£** denotes lower charges.

ISTANBUL
life

A PERSONAL VIEW

Connections

In November 1996 a car crash on the six-lane Istanbul highway involving a lorry and a dark blue Mercedes travelling at high speed led to a national scandal when it was discovered that the occupants of the car were a former deputy police chief, a terrorist of the far right, a former beauty queen turned gangsters' moll and a member of parliament belonging to the prime minister's True Path Party. Government-issue automatic weapons and a variety of listening devices were also found in the car. Following a clumsy attempt at a cover-up, the Minister of Interior was forced to resign while parliament debated government links with organised crime.

Istanbul wakes at dawn to the cries of the muezzin calling the faithful to prayer: '*Allah-u-ekber!*' ('God is great!') rings out across the rooftops, the throaty baritone voices boosted nowadays by loudspeakers attached to every minaret. Islam, the religion of the vast majority of people here, dictates the rhythm of the day. The urgent call is heard four times more: at midday, in the afternoon, at sunset and again after dark. It is an unforgettable experience to sail into the Golden Horn at dusk as the chant breaks out and the sun dissolves into a red haze behind the domes and minarets of the four hundred mosques of the city.

Istanbul lies on the Bosphorus, a narrow stretch of water 30km long which acts as a natural frontier between Europe and Asia – it takes time to get used to the ease with which one can cross continents here. The city's strategic importance led the Emperor Constantine to make it the new capital of the Roman Empire in the 4th century AD and, when the Byzantine Empire fell more than a thousand years later, the Ottoman conquerors saw no reason to move elsewhere. The port is still at the heart of this maritime city.

Today, the Bosphorus, linking the Black Sea to the Mediterranean by way of the Sea of Marmara, has some of the world's busiest shipping lanes. Look out from the terrace of Topkapı Palace at any time of day and you will see oil tankers from Russia, Bulgaria and Azerbaijan massing like warships at the mouth of the Marmara, while sleek white cruise ships from Venice and Odessa line up along the shores of Beyoğlu.

The fairytale domes and minarets of the Sultanahmet Camii (Blue Mosque)

Beyoğlu is where Istanbul's shops, banks and offices are concentrated, attracting a vast army of commuters each morning. The dominant landmark is the conical Galata Tower, built by Genoese merchants in the 14th century. Below, washing hangs out to dry in the congested streets, which cling precariously to the hillside. Locals avoid the steep climb by taking the tiny underground railway, known as the Tünel. They emerge on İstiklâl Caddesi, one of Istanbul's few genuine avenues. Here, Western influence, always conspicuous, is most in evidence at night when the restaurants, cinemas and nightclubs are bathed in garish neon.

Back on the Eminönü waterfront the fishermen, some dressed in fezzes and embroidered jackets for the tourists, hand up steaming rolls of mackerel to passers by – lunch for busy Istanbullers, a mid-morning snack for others. Stop even for a moment and you will be besieged by shoe-shine boys, opportunist tour guides and dealers in boat tokens, combs, postcards, penny whistles, amulets to ward off the 'evil eye' and cigarettes – the sales pitch invariably prefixed by a hopeful 'Yes, please'. For the 300,000 new citizens arriving each year from the impoverished villages of

Entrepreneur

Abdulgani Geçmez is typical of Istanbul's thrusting young entrepreneurs. After working in a local carpet shop to learn the ropes, he set up in business with a friend in premises near the Blue Mosque. They already have plans to develop the export side of the business, especially in the US. What makes these 'Young Turks' remarkable is their insistence on the quality of the product and a willingness to work into the small hours to promote it.

Commuters

The area of old Istanbul known as the Beyazıt–Sirkeci–Eminönü triangle has a remarkably transient population. Each day an estimated 800,000 people arrive for work in the handicraft shops, government offices, small businesses and tourist sights. At night, however, the district is all but deserted as the workers return to their homes in the suburbs, leaving the visitors to drink in the numerous bars and restaurants.

Bustling Beyazıt Square

Anatolia, street trading is the only way to eke out a living and maybe send a small sum to the family back home. They sleep in the wretched *gecekondu* (shanty towns) on the outskirts of the city, but during the day their haunts are the main tourist sights of Eminönü: Ayasofya, the Sultanahmet Camii, Topkapı Palace and so on.

Istanbul's 18,000 taxi-drivers seem as thick on the ground as the street traders. This must be one of the few cities where cab-drivers will find you rather than the other way round. If you get lost in one of the backstreets behind the Covered Bazaar, don't panic. The odds are that one of Istanbul's ubiquitous yellow cabs will be waiting for you at the next corner, the door already open. In a city with such a chaotic public transport system, the taxi is the only serious way to get about (with the honourable exception of the ferry). Fares are reasonable and your driver will know all the shortcuts – there's no more reliable person to get you safely back to your hotel.

But it's the ferry that you will fall in love with. No ride costs more than a couple of dollars and there's no better cure for a case of the sightseeing blues than to jump on a boat bound for the Bosphorus. The options are endless. You can take the commuter ferry to Üsküdar, have lunch in one of Ortaköy's legendary fish restaurants or take a stroll through the woods of Yıldız Park – a lovers' lane for young Istanbullers. At the weekend, locals leave the city to go picnicking on the shores of the Bosphorus. If you ferry-hop, you can catch up with them beneath the romantic ruins of Anadolu Hisarı castle, in the wooded hills of Beykoz or enjoying the views from the cafés of Kanlıca or Sarıyer.

ISTANBUL IN FIGURES

GEOGRAPHY
- Istanbul is the only city built on two continents
- At 41°02N, 28°57E, Istanbul is on a similar latitude to Beijing, Madrid and New York
- Istanbul covers approximately 5,712sq km
- Atatürk International Airport is 2,497km from London, 2,240km from Paris, 1,755km from Moscow, 9,260km from Tokyo, 8,059km from New York, 445km from Bucharest and 488km from Sofya

POPULATION
- AD 530 – 400,000 (estimated)
- 1400 – 50,000
- 1900 –1,000,000
- 1990 – 6,620,000 (trebled in three decades)
- 1997 – 9,792,000 (estimated; including surrounding conurbation, nearer 12 million)
- Istanbul is the largest city in Turkey

ISTANBUL HAS
- Over 1 million registered vehicles, 20 per cent of all those registered in Turkey
- 18,000 yellow taxis
- 1,000 carpet shops in Covered Bazaar alone
- 18 daily newspapers and 13 weeklies
- A literacy rate of over 90 per cent
- 870,000 visitors to Topkapı Palace
- 650,000 visitors to Ayasofya
- 2,555,000 visitors to the Covered Bazaar

COMMERCE
- Istanbul's GNP per capita is almost twice the national average
- Istanbul's chief industries are the port, textiles, shipbuilding, food processing, leather, tobacco and tourism
- 242 out of Turkey's top 500 companies are located in Istanbul

HISTORY
- Constantinople was an imperial capital for a total of 1,593 years
- It is the only city in the world to have been the capital of Christian and Muslim empires
- In 1547 there were 77 Christian churches
- It faced 20 sieges beween AD 441 and 1453
- It had 109 great fires between 1633 and 1854
- It suffered six major earthquakes: in AD 212, 478, 553, 1509, 1766 and 1894

A CHRONOLOGY

667 BC	Byzantium founded by the Megarian leader, Byzas, at Sarayburnu (Seraglio Point)
133 BC	Byzantium becomes part of the Roman province of Asia after the last ruler of Pergamon surrenders his kingdom
11 May AD 330	The Emperor Constantine decrees that Byzantium is to be the new capital of the Roman Empire
395	On the death of Theodosius I the Roman Empire is officially divided into two. Byzantium (now known as Constantinople) becomes the capital of the Eastern Roman Empire
412–22	Theodosius II orders the building of a new wall around the city
527–65	The reign of the Emperor Justinian begins. The Eastern Roman Empire flourishes, extending its influence from Spain to Iran
26 Dec 537	Dedication of the church of Ayasofya
1204	Constantinople is sacked during the Fourth Crusade
1396	The Ottoman Sultan Yıldırım Bayezid builds a fortress at Anadolu Hisarı on the Bosphorus, threatening Constantinople directly for the first time
29 May 1453	Constantinople falls to Sultan Mehmet II (the 'Conqueror') after a siege lasting seven weeks
***c.* 1459–65**	Building of the Topkapı Palace
1617	Building of the Sultanahmet Mosque
1683	Ottoman expansion is finally halted and the fortunes of the empire begin to decline
1839	Sultan Abdülmecid and his prime minister, Mustafa Reşid, proclaim the Tanzimat

('Reorganisation'). The reforms include
promises of greater consultation, a more equi-
table taxation system and equal treatment
before the law for Muslims and non-Muslims

1853 | Sultan Abdülmecit moves out of Topkapı
Palace and into Dolmabahçe

1875 | Opening of underground funicular railway
known as the Tünel

1889 | The railway from Europe finally reaches
Istanbul's Sirkeci station, and the legendary
Orient Express goes into service

1894 | Istanbul experiences its most recent major
earthquake

1909 | Young Turk reformers depose Sultan
Abdülhamit II and restore parliament and the
constitution, but the reforms are quickly
abrogated

1914 | Turkey enters World War I on the side of
Germany, a decision which ultimately proves
disastrous

1919 | As the defeated Ottoman government is
compelled by the Allies to sign the humiliating
Treaty of Sèvres, Mustafa Kemal Paşa (Atatürk)
embarks on a national war of liberation

29 Oct 1923 | The Turkish National Assembly proclaims the
founding of a Turkish Republic with Atatürk as
President. Ankara becomes the new capital

10 Nov 1938 | Atatürk dies in Dolmabahçe Palace. The entire
country goes into mourning

1939–45 | Turkey remains neutral during World War II

1995 | Opening of new Istanbul Stock Exchange at
İstinye on the Bosphorus

1 Jan 1996 | Turkey enters into a customs union with the
European Union

11

PEOPLE & EVENTS FROM HISTORY

Roman Emperor Constantine the Great (AD 288–337)

The 'Lawgiver'

Arguably the most successful Ottoman sultan was Süleyman the Magnificent, known to the Turks as Kanuni, meaning the 'Lawgiver'. He was also a great builder, administrator and artistic patron, but it was his foreign exploits that made him a legend among his enemies. By the end of his 46-year reign Istanbul had become the capital of the most powerful state in the world, with territory stretching from the Aegean to North Africa and the Balkans, and a naval fleet that ruled the waves.

CONSTANTINE THE GREAT

Constantine's connection with the city that was to bear his name for more than a thousand years began in AD 324 when he defeated his imperial rival, Licinius, in the hills above Chrysopolis (now Üsküdar). As the ruler of a reunited Roman Empire, Constantine decided for strategic reasons to establish a 'new Rome' on the shores of the Bosphorus. The city was officially rededicated on 11 May 330 and, shortly afterwards, renamed Constantinopolis in honour of Rome's first Christian emperor.

MEHMET THE CONQUEROR

Mehmet II came to the throne at the age of 19 in 1451 and immediately made plans to capture Constantinople. The siege began in April with a massive artillery bombardment of the city's land walls. Mehmet was assisted by European ballistics experts, who had constructed the largest cannon in the world with a barrel more than 7m long. After two failed attempts to take the city, his forces finally breached the walls on 29 May 1453. Mehmet died in 1481, probably poisoned by his physician on the orders of his son, Bayezid II.

KEMAL ATATÜRK

Born in Salonika in 1880, Mustafa Kemal was an army officer who became a national hero after defeating the Allied forces at Gallipoli in 1915. Following Turkey's defeat in World War I and the partitioning of the Ottoman Empire, Kemal led a war of independence which succeeded, in the space of three years, in expelling all the occupying foreign forces from the Turkish heartland. As President of the Turkish Republic from 1923 until his death in 1938, Kemal transformed the country, introducing sweeping social reforms that gave women the vote, abolished religious courts, introduced the Western calendar and replaced the Arabic script with the Roman alphabet – all measures designed to promote the goal of modernisation. In 1934, to great popular acclaim, the President adopted the surname Atatürk, meaning 'Father of the Turks', a singularly appropriate epithet.

ISTANBUL
how to organise your time

ITINERARIES

Istanbul has so much to offer the tourist that planning your sightseeing can
be a daunting prospect. These four one-day itineraries will help guide you
to some of the major historic sights.

ITINERARY ONE	FROM AT MEYDANI (HIPPODROME) TO MISIR ÇARŞISI (SPICE BAZAAR)
Morning	Stroll northwards through the At Meydanı (Hippodrome; ► 36) Stop for coffee at one of the cafés on the square before visiting the Sultanahmet Camii (► 38) On leaving the mosque, cross Mimar Mehmet Ağa Caddesi, then walk through the Sultanahmet Park to Ayasofya Camii (Haghia Sophia; ► 40)
Lunch	House of Medusa Café Restaurant (► 68)
Afternoon	Pick up a tram on Alemdar Caddesi to Eminönü. Cross Reşadiye Caddesi and walk around the Yeni Camii (► 51) to sample the aromas of the Mısır Çarşısı (Spice Bazaar; ► 32) Return to Eminönü and cross the Galata Bridge, then take the Tünel from the corner of Evren Caddesi and Mertebani Sokak and alight at the terminus. Walk down Galip Dede Caddesi to the Galata Tower (► 58)
ITINERARY TWO	EMINÖNÜ, BOĞAZIÇI (BOSPHORUS) & ANADOLU KAVAĞI
Morning	Take a tram (or cross the Galata Bridge) to the Eminönü terminus. Buy a ticket for the round-trip ferry from the window at jetty 3. Refreshments are available on board. Look out for Dolmabahçe Sarayı (► 45), Yıldız Parkı (► 46), Ortaköy Camii (► 51) Beylerbeyi Sarayı (► 48) and Rumeli Hisarı (► 54). Disembark at Anadolu Kavağı (► 58)
Lunch	Eat in any of the fish restaurants in this attractive harbour
Afternoon	Climb the hill behind the village to the castle ruins of Anadolu Kavağı. Return to Eminönü on the ferry

ITINERARY THREE	**YEREBATAN SARAYI (BASILICA CISTERN) & TOPKAPI**
Morning	Go east along ancient Divan Yolu (► 52) to the Yerebatan Sarayı (Basilica Cistern; ► 37) in Sultanahmet Square. Take a subterranean coffee break in the Cistern café (► 68) Return to ground level, then follow Alemdar Caddesi to Gülhane Park. At the park gate, turn right along Soğukçeşme Sokak (► 52), admiring the picturesque wooden houses On reaching the fountain of Ahmet III (► 59), turn left through the entrance of Topkapı Sarayı (► 42) Stop to admire the ancient church of Aya İrini (► 50) in the First Courtyard before buying a ticket to the palace at the Babüsselâm Gate (entrance to Second Courtyard)
Lunch	Konyalı restaurant (Fourth Courtyard; ► 62)
Afternoon	Before visiting the palace museums, buy your ticket to the Harem to avoid queuing
ITINERARY FOUR	**KARIYE CAMII, SÜLEYMANIYE CAMII & KAPALI ÇARŞI (COVERED BAZAAR)**
Morning	Take a taxi to the Kariye Camii (► 27) After enjoying the wonderful mosaics and frescos in this celebrated old Byzantine church, linger over a coffee in the square Walk towards Fevzipaşa Caddesi and pick up a taxi for the Süleymaniye Camii (► 28)
Lunch	Darüzziyaf restaurant in the restored 16th-century mosque kitchens (► 66)
Afternoon	Don't leave the Süleymaniye without exploring the other precinct buildings, which include several *medreses* (religious colleges), Süleyman's mausoleum and the 'Street of Opium Addicts' (Tiryaki Çarşısı) Walk down Fuat Paşa Caddesi, past the University, and continue into Çadırcılar Caddesi, turning left into the famous Kapalı Çarşı (Covered Bazaar; ► 30)

WALKS

THE SIGHTS

- Yeni Camii (► 51)
- Rüstem Paşa Camii
  (► 31)
- Mısır Çarşısı (Spice
  Bazaar; ► 32)
- Mahmutpaşa Yokuşu
- Mahmutpaşa Camii
- Mahmutpaşa Baths
- Nuruosmaniye Camii
  (► 51)
- Kapalı Çarşı (Covered
  Bazaar; ► 30)

INFORMATION

Distance 1.5km
Time 3 hours
Start point Eminönü
   terminus
🚋 K12
🚇 Eminönü
End point Kapalı Çarşı
   (Covered Bazaar)
🚋 L12
🚇 Beyazıt

Busy Eminönü street

TWO BAZAARS

Cross Reşadiye Caddesi via the underpass to the Yeni Camii. When the mosque was founded in the 17th century it stood on the seashore and had to be underpinned by wooden posts. The income to support the mosque was provided by the Spice Bazaar. Continue along the main road (now Sobacılar Caddesi) to one of Sinan's finest creations, the 16th-century Rüstem Paşa Camii. Take time to admire the beautiful tiled interior and perhaps stop for coffee in one of the shops beneath the terrace. Walk eastwards along Hasırcılar Caddesi to the Tahmis Gate of the Mısır Çarşısı (Spice Bazaar). You'll be tempted to linger here, attracted by the wonderful aromas and the colourful fruits and spices.

Leave by the Çiçek Pazarı Gate and cross into Saka Mehmet Sokak, leading to Küçük Sokak. Turn left into Mahmutpaşa Yokuşu. This hilly street is always swarming with people, attracted by the market which operates from Monday to Saturday. Here the shop fronts spill out onto the pavement, engulfed by layer on layer of cheap clothing and fabrics. Just off to your right you will see the dome of the Mahmutpaşa Baths. Enter below the large yellow sign and you will find the original 15th-century chambers, for the time being occupied by street traders.

Return to Mahmutpaşa Yokuşu and turn left into Kücük Yıldız Hanı Sokak. On your left is the Mahmutpaşa Camii, which dates back to the time of Mehmet the Conqueror. Walk down Kılıççılar Sokak, then turn left into Çarşıkapı Nuruosmaniye Sokak, past the Nuruosmaniye Camii to the gate of the same name which leads into the Kapalı Çarşı (Covered Bazaar). End your walk here with a coffee.

EXPLORING THE LAND WALLS

Take a taxi to Tekfur Sarayı on Şişehane
Caddesi. The 'museum director', as she
likes to be called, will take time off from
her washing to point the way to the ruins
(for a small consideration). Tekfur Sarayı
(Palace of the Sovereign) dates from the
end of the 13th century. You can climb to
the ramparts for fabulous views across the
Golden Horn.

*Byzantine ruins of the
Tekfur Sarayı*

After leaving Tekfur Sarayı, turn left (away from
the walls) onto Çakırağa Yokuşu. Turn right at
the yellow church of Panayia Hançeriotissa
Kilisesi – it originally dates from the Byzantine
period although the present building is 19th-
century (the fountain in the courtyard is also
Byzantine). Continue along Kariye Türbesi
Sokak to Kariye Meydanı, where you'll see the
famous Kariye Camii and, near by, the spruce-
looking Kariye Hotel and Café. Many of the
19th-century wooden houses here have been
restored. Take time to admire the breathtaking
frescos and mosaics in the former Byzantine
church before continuing south along Kariye
Camii Sokak into Şeyh Eyüp Sokak. Cross the
main road, Fevzi Paşa Caddesi, and walk
towards Edirne Kapısı. It was through this gate
that Mehmet the Conqueror entered the city
on 29 May 1453 after the Janissaries had
breached the adjoining walls.

Turn south onto Hocaçakır Caddesi to the
Mihrimah Sultan Camii (1562). On leaving the
mosque, turn left and follow Hocaçakır
Caddesi/Sulukule Caddesi along the land
walls. Cross busy Adnan Menderes
Caddesi and continue in the shadow
of the walls along Sulukule
Caddesi to Topkapı, the
famous 'Cannon Gate',
also breached by the
Conqueror in 1453.
Here you will find a
taxi rank and several
transport cafés.

THE SIGHTS

- Tekfur Sarayı (➤ 24)
- Panayia Hançeriotissa
  Kilisesi
- Kariye Camii (➤ 27)
- Edirne Kapısı
- Mihrimah Sultan Camii
  (➤ 26)
- Topkapı (Cannon Gate)

INFORMATION

Distance 2.5km
Time 2–3 hours
Start point Tekfur Sarayı
✚ H9
End point Topkapı (Cannon
  Gate)
✚ K8
🚊 Ulubatı
🚌 Topkapı

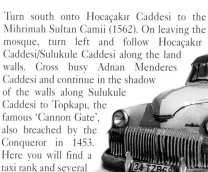

17

EVENING STROLLS

INFORMATION

İstiklâl Caddesi
Distance 1½km
Time 1 hour
Start point Taksim Meydanı
🚌 G13
🚋 İstiklâl Caddesi (Taksim Meydanı)
End point Tünel station
🚌 J12
🚋 Tünel

ISTIKLÂL CADDESI

Ask your taxi-driver to drop you off at Taksim Meydanı. Pay your respects to the marble Monument to the Republic in the centre of the square before turning down İstiklâl Caddesi. Here you will rub shoulders with Istanbul's night crowd, heading for the restaurants, bars, clubs and cinemas that are crammed into the neighbouring seedy sidestreets. Pass the old octagonal water fountain (now a tourist information office), the French Consulate and the Ağa Camii, and you will come to Çiçek Pasajı, a *belle époque* arcade lined with some of the city's liveliest *meyhanes* (taverns) and resounding to the strains of oriental music. Beyond Galatasaray Square and the ornate gateway of Istanbul's most prestigious *lycée*, İstiklâl quietens down. Continue past the pseudo-Renaissance façade of St Anthony's Catholic Church and the Four Seasons restaurant, and you will find the entrance to the celebrated Tünel funicular, which will take you down to the Galata Bridge.

Sunset over the Golden Horn and Eyüp Sultan Camii

ÜSKÜDAR WATERFRONT

Take the ferry from Eminönü (Sirkeci İskelesi) to Harem İskelesi on the Asian shore. To the rear of the landing stage, off Selimiye İskele, is the barracks where the famous British nurse, Florence Nightingale, set up her hospital during the Crimean War. Stroll northwards along Harem Sahil Yolu. There are fine views from here – you should be able to pick out the domes and minarets of Ayasofya and Sultanahmet Camii, the ancient sea walls and, above them, Topkapı Palace. On an island out in the Bosphorus the 18th-century lighthouse Kız Kulesi (Maiden's Tower) will gradually come into view. On the hill above the dominant landmark is the Ayazma Camii, a Baroque masterpiece by Mehmet Tahir Ağa. The road now winds into Üsküdar, passing the *külliye* of the exquisite Şemsi Paşa Camii. On reaching the town you will find cafés and local *meyhanes*.

Üsküdar Waterfront
Distance 2½km
Time 1–2 hours
Start point Harem İskelesi
🚌 L16
⛴ Harem
End point Üsküdar
🚌 J16
⛴ Üsküdar

ORGANISED SIGHTSEEING

ALTERNATIF TURIZM
Walking and mountain-biking tours around Istanbul; also trekking, rafting, paragliding and canoeing tours in the region.

✉ Bağdat Caddesi 36/8, Kızıltoprak ☎ (216) 345 6650

ARNIKA
Organises daily and weekend tours in the country-side surrounding Istanbul.

✉ İstiklâl Caddesi, Mis Sokak 6/5, Beyoğlu ☎ 245 1593

FEST
Deals in specialised cultural tours around the less-known corners of Istanbul and the region.

✉ Barbaros Bulvarı 85/AD13, Beşiktaş ☎ 258 2589

FOTOĞRAF EVI
This photography and travel club organises weekend nature walks for photography enthusiasts; also hosts exhibitions and video shows.

✉ İstiklâl Caddesi, Zambak Sokak 15, 4th floor, Beyoğlu
☎ 251 0566

GENÇTUR
Organises weekend 'green' tours in the Istanbul area.

✉ Yerebatan Caddesi 15/3, Sultanahmet ☎ 520 5274

GÖÇERLER PHOTOGRAPHY CLUB
Organises tours around Istanbul and the region for nature and photography enthusiasts.

✉ Miralay Nazim Sokak 36/3, Kadıköy ☎ (216) 414 4474

GRUP GÜNBATMADAN
'Before Sunset Travels' will arrange trekking trips around Istanbul and the region, catering to all levels and age groups.

✉ İstiklâl Caddesi, Zambak Sokak 15, 4th floor, Beyoğlu ☎ 245 5954

PLAN TOURS
Daily tours around Istanbul and the region. Also private yacht cruises on the Bosphorus.

✉ Cumhuriyet Caddesi 131/1, Elmadağ ☎ 230 2272

Guides

You can hire an official English-speaking guide at any of the tourist information offices or you can try one of the many travel agencies on Divan Yolu. Some of the larger hotels are also happy to help. Turkish guides usually speak more than adequate English and are experienced at showing people around. You will also find any number of freelance guides around major sights like Ayasofya and Topkapı Palace.

Süleymaniye Camii

EXCURSIONS

Trotsky

The most famous 20th-century exile on the Princes' Islands was the Russian revolutionary Leon Trotsky. Deported by Stalin in 1929, he received permission from President Atatürk to settle on Büyükada, where he lived until 1933. You can visit his home on 55 Çankaya Caddesi.

BELGRADE FOREST

Belgrade Forest has an intriguing network of aqueducts, reservoirs and water channels created by the architect Sinan in the 16th century at the behest of his master, Süleyman the Magnificent. The forest takes its name from the Serbian prisoners of war brought here to supervise the installations after the Ottoman capture of Belgrade in 1521. Sinan built more than 30 aqueducts, mainly on Roman and Byzantine foundations. The most accessible to visitors are the Büyük Bend Reservoir, easily reached from Bahçeköy, and the Uzunkemer Reservoir near Kemerburgaz, a magnificent, two-tier structure, 713m long and 26m high. Scenic woodland paths thread through the forest and there's a picnic area at Neşet Suyu. The forest is busiest at weekends when Istanbullers come here to escape the city pollution.

PRINCES' ISLANDS

The Princes' Islands form an archipelago off the Asian coast of the Sea of Marmara and have been inhabited since classical times – one of Alexander the Great's generals built a fort here in the 3rd century BC. In the Byzantine era the many monasteries served as prisons for exiled members of the imperial family. Sparsely populated until modern times, the islands are now Istanbul's most fashionable holiday resort. The boat calls at four of them: Kınalıada, Burgazda, Heybeliada and Büyükada. Motor traffic is prohibited but you can hire a pony and trap or bicycle to get around. There are sandy coves and wonderful walks across the clifftops and through the pine forests. On your way you can stop to admire the *yalıs* (wooden summer mansions) belonging to the rich and famous. Some visitors however, never make it past the fish restaurants which line every seafront.

Transport on Heybeliada, Princes' Islands

BAYRAMOĞLU BIRD PARK AND BOTANIC GARDENS

A paradise for wildlife enthusiasts and ideal for children, Bayramoğlu was founded in 1991 primarily to protect endangered species of birds. The park, which covers some 14 hectares, opened to the public two years later. Among the 350 species of birds are ara and kakadu parrots, toucans, peacocks, ostriches, lorikeets, cranes, herons, flamingos, storks, eagles and snowy owls, all held in specially re-created 'natural' habitats. In the animal compounds, you will find llamas, miniature silk monkeys and some ferocious-looking alligators, as well as Buba, the retired circus bear. If your children balk at the Botanic Gardens, you can bribe them with the promise of a visit to the playground afterwards.

KILYOS

The seaside resort of Kilyos lies on the European shores of the Black Sea. The journey from Sarıyer is part of the fun – you share the *dolmuş* with local villagers. As the road threads across the backs of the surrounding hills there are superb views of the Bosphorus while the Black Sea shimmers in the distance. Kilyos boasts only one sight, a clifftop castle built by the Genoese in the Middle Ages; nowadays it's an army base and strictly off-limits to tourists. Below are long stretches of clean sand and a sprinkling of unpretentious cafés and restaurants. Should you miss the last *dolmuş*, there are several hotels in the village (see panel) or you can take a taxi back (ask in the local store).

INFORMATION

Bayramoğlu Bird Park and Botanic Gardens
Distance 38km
Journey time 1 hour
✉ Darıca Kuş Cenneti, Darıca
☎ (262) 653 1374
🍴 Café
🚌 Municipal bus
💵 Moderate
🎁 Gift shop

Kilyos
Distance 30km
Journey time 45 mins
🍴 Cafés and restaurants
🚌 *Dolmuş* to Kilyos from Sarıyer, or municipal bus
ℹ Recommended Kilyos hotels: Kilyos Kale (☎ 201 1818); Turban Kilyos Moteli (☎ 201 1480)

Kilyos, Istanbul's closest beach resort

WHAT'S ON

For confirmation of dates and programmes, contact the Istanbul tourist information offices (► 90) or the Atatürk Cultural Center (► 78). For other information, see *Istanbul the Guide*, published bi-monthly, and *Informist*, an annual publication containing details of trade fairs and exhibitions in Istanbul.

MARCH/APRIL	*International Film Days*: cinemas feature new releases of Turkish and foreign films as well as retrospectives and historic films
APRIL	*National Sovereignty and Children's Day* (23 Apr): a celebration with parades and processions by school children *Tulip Festival*: in Emirgan Park
MAY	*Youth and Sports Day* (19 May): sports parades and displays marking Atatürk's birthday *International Theatre Festival* *Fatih Day* (29 May): festivities celebrating the conquest of the city in 1453 by Sultan Fatih Mehmet
JUNE	*International Regatta:* offshore races are held between Istanbul and the Aegean coastal city of Izmir
JUNE/JULY	*International Music Festival*: featuring international and home-grown stars of classical, jazz and rock music, opera, ballet and folk dancing. Many of the concerts are held in beautiful or historic settings, such as the grounds of Rumeli Hisarı and the Byzantine church of Aya İrini
JULY	*International Jazz Festival*
AUGUST	*Victory Day* (30 Aug): parades take place down the main streets – an opportunity to see the few surviving veterans of the War of Independence
OCTOBER	*Autumn Akbank Jazz Festival* *Republic Day* (28–9 Oct): patriotic displays and fireworks marking the anniversary of the proclamation of the Republic in 1923
NOVEMBER	*Anniversary of Atatürk's death* (10 Nov): a minute's silence is observed all over the city at 09:05 (the exact time of Atatürk's death)

ISTANBUL's
top 25 sights

The sights are shown on the maps on the inside front cover and inside back cover, numbered **1–25** *from west to east across the city*

1

YEDIKULE

DID YOU KNOW?

- The land walls stretch for a total distance of 6.5km
- The inner walls are 5m thick and 12m high, and have 96 towers spaced at 50–70m intervals
- The outer walls are 9m thick and 8.5m high, and also have 96 towers
- There are seven main gates

INFORMATION

- N7 (Yedikule) to H9 (Tekfur Sarayı)
- Yedikule Meydanı Sokak
- 585 8933
- Tue–Sun 9:30–4:30
- Cafés (£) near by
- Yedikule
- None
- Cheap

"It is possible to spend a whole day exploring the old Byzantine fortifications, with their watchtowers, gateways and parapets. Access is virtually unrestricted, and if you are able and willing to climb you will be rewarded with superb views of the city and the Sea of Marmara."

The land walls Stretching all the way from the Sea of Marmara to the Golden Horn, Constantinople's land walls enclosed the entire Byzantine city. They were built in AD 412–22 during the reign of Theodosius II, and apart from severe structural damage sustained during an earthquake in 447 survived almost intact until they were finally breached in 1453 by Sultan Mehmet the Conqueror.

Yedikule Castle The Fortress of the Seven Towers assumed its present form around 1460 when Mehmet added five towers to the Porta Aurea (Golden Gate). Dating from 390, this was originally a free-standing triumphal arch used exclusively by emperors to enter the city. The gate still exists although the gold-plated doors and statues have long since disappeared and the arches themselves have been bricked up. First used as a treasury, the castle became a place of imprisonment as notorious as the Bastille in Paris. Among its victims were foreign ambassadors held as hostages, Ottoman politicians and members of the ruling dynasty. In one of the towers is the cell where, in 1622, the deposed sultan, Osman II, was murdered by the traditional method of strangulation by bowstring – his testicles were crushed simultaneously to add to the torment. You can also see the Well of Blood into which severed heads were unceremoniously tossed. At the far end of the walls are the ruins of the 13th-century Tekfur Sarayı (Palace of the Sovereign).

Top: Theodosian land walls and Yedikule Castle

EYÜP SULTAN CAMII

"*The best time to visit Eyüp is on holy days (including Friday prayers) when crowds of pilgrims descend on this famous shrine to make their devotions. The market stalls do a brisk trade in evil-eye amulets, koranic plates and other religious ephemera.***"**

Shrine Eyüp Ensari, standard-bearer and close companion of the Prophet Muhammad, fell in battle during the Arab siege of Constantinople in AD 674–8. His burial place was rediscovered in 1453 by Akşemseddin, tutor of Mehmet the Conqueror, and the delighted sultan erected a shrine on the site.

Mosque and *türbe* (mausoleum) The original mosque was destroyed during the earthquake of 1766 and rebuilt by Selim III. A fine example of Ottoman baroque, the interior is highlighted with gold leaf on white marble and graced by a sumptuous turquoise carpet, the gift of a former Turkish premier. In the courtyard young boys play chase around the plane trees, and pigeons scurry beneath the fountain. After praying at the mosque, pious Muslims make their way to the octagonal mausoleum of Eyüp Ensari. Dating from 1485, the *türbe* is decorated with blue, white and henna-red tiles from İznik and Kütahya. Worshippers pause at the 'wishing window' (protected by a golden grille) before filing past the sarcophagus. Preserved in one corner is a cast of the Prophet Muhammad's footprint.

Cemetery Take time to explore some of the other mausoleums that line the 'street of tombs' behind the mosque. A stroll through the hillside cemetery, its faded marble tombstones and crooked stelae half-hidden by cypresses, is a perfect way to round off a visit.

HIGHLIGHTS

- ● Gold-leaf decoration
- ● Mosque courtyard
- ● Tiles on mausoleum
- ● Wishing window
- ● Mausoleum of Ferhat Paşa
- ● Mausoleum of Siyavuş Paşa
- ● Prophet's footprint

Eyüp Sultan Camii

INFORMATION

- ✛ F8
- ✉ Camii Kebir Caddesi, Eyüp
- 🕒 Mosque: hours of prayer. Mausoleum of Eyüp: Tue–Sun 9:30–4:30
- 🍴 Pierre Loti Café (££; panel ➤ 58)
- 🚢 Eyüp Vapur İskelesi
- ♿ None
- 💷 Free
- ❓ No photographs in Eyüp mausoleum

25

MIHRIMAH SULTAN CAMII

HIGHLIGHTS

- 200 plain and stained-glass windows
- Marble mimbar
- Arabesque stencilling
- Central dome
- Garden courtyard
- Fountain in courtyard
- Mausoleum of Semiz Ali Paşa
- Street bazaar under terrace

INFORMATION

- H9
- Fevzi Paşa Caddesi, Fatih
- Hours of prayer
- Cafés (£) near by
- None
- Free
- Land walls and Tekfur Sarayı (▶ 24), Kariye Camii (▶ 27)

Top: the soaring hall is flooded with light
Below: a prototype of mosque design

" *What is really astonishing about the Mihrimah Mosque is the impression of light flooding in from all directions, as row upon row of stained-glass windows throw beams of turquoise, pink, blue and gold across the central prayer hall. This is what makes the mosque an all-time favourite of ours.* **"**

Sultan's daughter The patron of this beautiful mosque, Mihrimah Sultan, was the favourite daughter of Süleyman the Magnificent and the richest woman in the world at the time. She shared a passion for architecture with her husband, Rüstem Paşa, and they were both important patrons of Sinan, the great builder.

Sinan's prototype With the Mihrimah Sultan Mosque, Sinan ingeniously created a prototype for mosque design that was to endure through-out the Ottoman era. The centrepiece is the enormous cuboid prayer hall, entirely covered by a dome 36.5m high and 20m across. The wonderful sense of space is achieved by banish-ing the galleries to a series of domed bays at the north and south ends. With this uninterrupted view, visitors can appreciate the magnificence of the decoration as they look upwards to the arabesque stencilling between the supporting arches and across to the multi-coloured tiling of the mihrab wall. The marble mimbar, one of the finest of its kind, is also the work of Sinan.

Contrasts While the terrace overlooking Istanbul's highest hill, the Edirne Kapı, conceals a bustling *arasta* (street bazaar), the garden courtyard, in complete contrast, is a haven of quiet and contemplation. Within these colonnades you will find the *türbe* of Semiz Ali Paşa (Mihrimah's son-in-law), as well as a delightful ablution fountain.

KARIYE CAMII

❝The lovely old Church of St Saviour of Chora is a must-see as it houses one of the world's most precious collections of Byzantine mosaics and frescos. The dramatic rendering of the Resurrection in the apse seems to speak directly to us across the gulf of nearly seven centuries.**❞**

Metochites' church The Church of St Saviour in Chora (now the Kariye Camii Museum) was built between 1316 and 1321, and incorporates the shell of an earlier 12th-century church. *Chora* means 'in the country', an allusion to an even older foundation, which stood outside the city walls. The church's patron was Metochites, a distinguished Byzantine scholar and statesman who served the Emperor Andronicus II Palaelogus as prime minister and treasurer. When the emperor was overthrown in 1328, Metochites also fell from power and was sent into exile. Two years later he was allowed to return as a monk to live out his days in the confines of the church he had founded.

Mosaics and frescos Fortunately, the glory of the church, its mosaics and frescos were not destroyed when the building was converted into a mosque in 1511. They represent the late flowering of Byzantine art and are almost certainly the work of a single unknown artist, who left his signature in the hooked tails of the drapery and the peculiar 'shadows' around the feet. The mosaics are ambitious narrative cycles depicting the life and ministry of Christ and the life of the Virgin Mary. Above the door leading into the nave is a representation of Metochites presenting his church to Christ; he is wearing the typical Byzantine sun hat known as a *skiadon*. The frescos are confined to the parekklesion and, as befits a mortuary chapel, depict the Last Judgement and the Harrowing of Hell.

HIGHLIGHTS

- Christ Pantocrator (mosaic)
- Miracle at Cana (mosaic)
- Metochites presenting Chora to Christ (mosaic)
- Tomb of Metochites
- Last Judgement (fresco)
- Resurrection (fresco)
- Mother of God (fresco)

Byzantine chapel detail

INFORMATION

- ✚ H9
- ✉ Kariye Camii Sokak, Edirnekapı
- ☎ 523 3009
- 🕐 Wed–Mon 9:30–4:30
- 🍴 Kariye Hotel café/restaurant (£££; ► 85)
- 🚫 None
- 🖊 Moderate
- ↔ Land walls (► 24), Mihrimah Sultan Camii (► 26)
- ❓ No flash photography. Museum shop

27

5

SÜLEYMANIYE CAMII

"*It's easy to be bowled over by Süleyman's sumptuous mausoleum in the mosque garden, but many visitors overlook the smaller and even more exquisitely decorated tomb of his beloved wife, Haseki Hürrem, better known in the West as Roxelana.***"**

Külliye With the construction of the Süleymaniye Mosque complex between 1550 and 1559, the architect Sinan finally emancipated himself from the influence of Ayasofya to reveal his astonishing originality. In the 16th century the entire compound would have hummed with human activity – within the precincts were four *medreses*, schools, public kitchens, shops, baths and a *caravanserai* where travellers were guaranteed three days free board and lodging. Life is gradually returning to the Süleymaniye as some of the buildings are being restored; the Evvel and Sani *medreses*, for example, have been converted into one of Istanbul's most important libraries, while the *imaret* is now a restaurant.

Interior The prayer hall is a perfect square, each side measuring 26.5m, while the diameter of the dome is exactly half its height. All the other elements in the composition – semi-domes and cupolas, window-lit tympana, galleries and pillars – dance in attendance around this crowning feature. There is little sculptural decoration, but Sinan has allowed his other artists free rein, especially on the mihrab wall with its coloured marbles, calligraphy and magnificent stained-glass windows. For once we know the identity of some of these artists: the calligrapher (who apparently went blind in the process) was Ahmet Karahisarı; the windows were designed by İbrahim Sarhoş ('the Drunkard'); the woodwork, inlaid with ivory and mother-of-pearl, is by Ustad Ahmed.

BEYAZIT MEYDANI & BAYEZID CAMII

"We recommend the square of Beyazıt Meydanı as one of the best places to feel the pulse of this tumultuous city. Here you'll find students and hawkers rubbing shoulders with the devout, while small boys kick footballs – and beg from tourists, given half the chance!"

The square Beyazıt Meydanı, one of Istanbul's busiest squares, occupies the site of the Forum Taurii, once a thriving Byzantine market-place – you can see some remains of it on the other side of Ordu Caddesi, part of the Roman street known as the Mese. Today, the square contains the ceremonial gateway to Istanbul University and the Bayezid Mosque *medrese*, now the Calligraphy Museum (▶ 55).

The mosque The graceful Bayezid Mosque was built between 1501 and 1506 in the reign of Bayezid II, known as 'Veli' (the 'Saint') on account of his religious zeal – he went so far as to close down all the city's taverns. You will find his *türbe* (mausoleum) in the cemetery behind the mosque. The architect of this magnificent complex, Yakub Şah, clearly had an eye for detail as well as an instinct for geometrical proportion. He uses these gifts to brilliant effect in the colonnaded courtyard, where the columns of contrasting red, grey and green marble are crowned with stalactite decoration. Yakub Şah modelled the interior on the Christian church of Ayasofya. Four massive piers support the central dome, which is flanked by two semi-domes. The mimbar, mihrab and beautifully sculptured balustrade are original 16th-century features, as is the sultan's loge, to the right of the mimbar, which rests on columns of precious marbles.

HIGHLIGHTS

- Book market
- University Gate
- Flea market
- *Medrese* (Calligraphy Museum; ▶ 55)
- Forum Taurii ruins
- Mosque: sculpted portico courtyard; 16th-century mimbar and balustrade
- Pigeon-food sellers

INFORMATION

- ✚ L11
- ✉ Beyazıt Meydanı
- ☎ Calligraphy Museum: 527 5851
- 🕐 Mosque: hours of prayer. Calligraphy Museum: Tue–Sat 9–4
- 🍴 Lively café scene in nearby streets (£)
- 🚇 Beyazıt
- ♿ None
- 💷 Free
- ↔ Süleymaniye Camii (▶ 28), Kapalı Çarşı (▶ 30), Şehzade Camii (▶ 51)

Tomb of Bayezid II

KAPALı ÇARŞı

"We like to visit the Covered Bazaar on Wednesdays when the carpet auction takes place in the Sandal Bedesten – the sale starts at about 1PM. It's fun to watch the dealers inspecting the merchandise for flaws before putting in their bids."

İç Bedesten The bazaar is a labyrinth of seemingly endless vaulted arcades and passageways lined with merchants selling their wares – a city within a city. At the heart of the market is the İç Bedesten, which dates from the period of the Ottoman conquest (1456–61). An enormous warehouse surrounded by market stalls and workshops, it was at one time protected from the elements by canvas awnings. Today, the İç Bedesten deals in Ottoman antiques, including firearms, old coins, copper and silverware.

Orientation Traditionally, certain streets specialise in the sale of particular items – Halıcılar Caddesi, for example, means 'Carpet-Sellers' Street'. If you are looking for leatherware, head for Keseciler Caddesi; if it's jewellery, gold and silverware you are after, try Kalpakçılar Caddesi. The range of goods on sale is astonishing: hand-painted bowls, brass lamps, embroidered waist-coats, T-shirts, kilim bags, meerschaum pipes and the ubiquitous amulets to ward off the 'evil eye'. Shopping in the bazaar can be tiring and you'll probably want to take a break in one of the many cafés, where you can join the traders taking tea or enjoying a game of backgammon.

Hans Don't leave the bazaar without taking a detour into the picturesque courtyards of the old *hans* or caravanserais, built originally to accommodate merchants. The ground floors of these arcaded buildings, once stables and storerooms, are now used as workshops.

RÜSTEM PAŞA CAMII

❝*This is the best place in Istanbul to learn to love the tile-maker's art. If you can, you should visit the gallery, where you will find examples of the architect Sinan's original designs that were considered too restrained by Rüstem Paşa.*❞

The mosque This little gem of a mosque dates from 1561. It was designed by the incomparable Sinan for Süleyman the Magnificent's son-in-law, Grand Vizier Rüstem Paşa, although he never lived to see it completed. The charitable institutions of the *külliye* were financed by the row of vaulted shops which Sinan constructed at street level below the expansive terrace that leads to the mosque itself. Space was at a premium in the city's commercial quarter, so the courtyard area is restricted to a delightful (and highly unusual) double porch. The sloping roof is supported by a row of delicately carved stone pillars.

Decoration Sinan planned the prayer hall as an octagon inscribed within a rectangle. The main dome is flanked by four semi-domes, one at each corner of the building, and rests on four massive octagonal columns and four pillars abutting on the east and west walls. There are galleries on the north and south sides. Following Rüstem Paşa's death, his widow, Mihrimah Sultan, spared no expense on the decoration of the mosque. Every available space on the walls, piers, pillars, galleries, mimbar and mihrab is set with exquisite İznik tiles, designed by artists from the palace's own workshops. While geometric motifs are in abundance, the predominant theme is the paradise garden, with delicately painted tulips, hyacinths and carnations appearing to sway in the breeze. The presence of 'Armenian red' in the colour scheme is a hallmark, indicating the high point of İznik tile production (1555–1620).

HIGHLIGHTS

- Terrace
- Double porch
- Carved stone capitals (porch)
- Lozenge capitals (prayer hall)
- Dome
- İznik tiles
- Octagonal columns
- Calligraphic shields under dome

INFORMATION

- ✚ K12
- ✉ Ragıp Gümüşpala Caddesi, Eminönü
- ◷ Hours of prayer
- 🍴 Cafés (£) near by
- 🚆 Eminönü
- 🚌 Eminönü
- ♿ None
- 💲 Free
- ↔ Mısır Çarşısı (▶ 32)

İznik tile decoration

9

Mısır Çarşısı

HIGHLIGHTS

- Pistachio-filled
  Turkish delight
- Apple tea
- Saffron
- Caviare from
  Azerbaijan
- *Pastırma* (cured,
  spiced beef)
- Nuts and dried fruit
- Brass pepper mills
- Gold and jewellery
  shops (panel ➤ 74)

INFORMATION

➕ K12

✉ Yeni Cami Caddesi,
  Eminönü

🕐 Mon–Sat 9–7

🍴 Pandeli restaurant (££;
  lunch only; ➤ 66)

🚌 Eminönü

🚢 Eminönü İskelesi

♿ None

💷 Free

🔄 Süleymaniye Camii
  (➤ 28), Rüstem Paşa
  Camii (➤ 31), Yeni
  Camii (➤ 51)

❝The Spice Bazaar makes for a more relaxing shopping trip than the Covered Bazaar because it's so much easier to find your way around. We like to see how many pieces of Turkish delight we can sample before the wily tradesmen trap us into buying some!❞

Egyptian Bazaar Completed in 1663 for Turhan Hatice Sultan, mother of Mehmet IV, the Spice Bazaar was intended to provide income for the charitable foundations of the nearby Yeni Mosque. The source of this income was the import duties levied on the spices as they passed through Egypt (then part of the Ottoman Empire), which is why the Turks still call this the Egyptian Bazaar.

Turkish delight The entrance to the bazaar is through one of four robust, double-arched gates. Of the 88 shops here today, only half a dozen specialise exclusively in herbs and spices; even so, the aroma is unmistakable, a heady mix of saffron, coriander, ginger, cinnamon, mint, paprika, sage and tamarind. The second overwhelming impression is the riot of colour. You will see hanging knots of aubergines, paprika and salamis, trays filled with sweets, nuts, dried figs and apricots, and counters stacked with red, yellow, blue and green pots of caviare from Russia, Iran and Azerbaijan. Few can resist the Turkish delight with its hazelnut and pistachio fillings; or the tea, scented with apples, oranges, lemons, cherries, cinnamon and rose-hip. If you are in the mood for an aphrodisiac, enquire at the dried fruit shop, Malatya Pazarı, or try the erotically named perfumes at Fuar Pazarı. And there can be no better way to round off a visit than to have lunch at the famous Pandeli restaurant – ask for one of the window seats overlooking the bazaar.

SOKULLU MEHMET PAŞA CAMII

"Istanbul's mosques are not only places of worship, but centres of religious education. In the courtyard of Sokullu Paşa you may well hear the rhythmic hum of schoolboys reciting the Koran in the medrese as they have done for centuries."

Sokullu Paşa Often overlooked by tourists, this small masterpiece by Mimar Sinan was commissioned by the Sultan's grand vizier, Sokullu Mehmet Paşa, in 1571–2. Born Bajica Sokolovic in Višegrad, Bosnia, in 1505, this formidable politician was successively falconer, grand admiral, vizier and viceroy of Europe before being appointed chief minister in 1565. His skills as a naval commander continued to recommend him to Süleyman's successors and, after rebuilding the Ottoman fleet, he scored a notable victory in the capture of Tunis in 1574. Sokullu Paşa dedicated the mosque which bears his name to his wife, İsmihan Sultan, daughter of Selim II.

Interior The prayer hall of this beautifully proportioned building is a model of taste and refinement. Sinan planned it as a hexagon within a rectangle, the unusually high dome supported at the corners by four smaller semi-domes. A low gallery around three sides of the hall rests on slender marble columns with characteristic Ottoman lozenge capitals. The chief glory of the mosque is the mihrab wall, stunningly arrayed in tiles from the İznik workshops. Swirling patterns of green and red tulips and carnations on a turquoise ground thrive in a visual context of pure white stone. Other outstanding features include some of the original painted arabesques under the gallery, fragments of black stone from the Kaaba in Mecca (above the entrance and in the mihrab wall) and the tiled crown on the mimbar, the only one of its kind in Istanbul.

HIGHLIGHTS

- Tiled cap of mimbar
- Tiles on mihrab wall
- Pointed arches in courtyard
- Fragments from the Kaaba
- Lozenge capitals
- Arabesque paintings under gallery
- Ablution fountain
- Faience panels above windows and doors
- Photographs of mosque sold by the guardian

INFORMATION

- M12
- Şehit Mehmet Paşa Sokak
- Hours of prayer
- None
- Free
- Kücük Ayasofya Camii (► 34), At Meydanı (► 36)

Top: the mihrab wall

33

11

KÜÇÜK AYASOFYA CAMII

HIGHLIGHTS

- Carved capitals on pillars
- Monogram of Justinian and Theodora on pillar
- Frieze honouring Justinian, Theodora and Sergius (under gallery)
- Remains of 6th-century marble facings
- 16th-century *medrese* cells
- Irregular octagonal nave
- First-floor gallery
- Cracks in walls caused by slippage

INFORMATION

- ✚ M12
- ✉ Mehmet Paşa Sokak, Kadırga
- 🕐 Hours of prayer
- ♿ None
- ✋ Free or gratuity
- ↔ Sokullu Mehmet Paşa Camii (► 33)
- ❓ Mosque guardian may act as a guide

"*This pearl of a church, almost certainly the oldest in Istanbul, has a most unusual design which has sometimes been put down to hurried workmanship but which we think only adds to the charm of the building.***"**

Christian beginnings The 'Little' Ayasofya Mosque is even older than the great Byzantine church which it resembles. It was commissioned by the Emperor Justinian in about AD 527 from the architect Anthemius of Tralles, who also worked on the Ayasofya church. It was converted to a mosque early in the 16th century, in the reign of Bayezid II, by the head of the Black Eunuchs, Hüseyin Ağa, who is buried in a tomb north of the apse. Damaged by earthquakes in 1648 and 1763, the mosque is currently suffering from subsidence caused by its proximity to the Sea of Marmara, although restoration work should be complete by the year 2000.

SS Sergius and Bacchus The Emperor Justinian chose two martyred Roman soldiers, Sergius and Bacchus, as patrons for his church. As a young man Justinian had been accused of treason; it is said that Sergius and Bacchus had saved his life by appearing in a dream to the Emperor Anastasius and proclaiming his innocence.

A Byzantine survivor If you look closely you will find plenty of evidence of the mosque's earlier history, from the intricately carved decoration on the column capitals, some of which bear Justinian's monogram, to the frieze under the gallery which, in Greek verse, honours the emperor, his consort Theodora and St Sergius, though curiously not Bacchus. There are also tell-tale traces of the original gold-leaf and marble revetments that once adorned the church.

Top: intricately carved
capitals and frieze

12

TÜRK VE ISLÂM ESERLERI MÜZESI

"Have you ever wondered how the carpet came to be an indispensable item of household furniture? Would you know how to go about making sheep's-milk cheese? All is revealed in the ethnography section of the Museum of Turkish and Islamic Art."

The palace The museum is housed in the former palace of Süleyman the Magnificent's grand vizier, İbrahim Paşa, who received it as a gift from the sultan in 1520.

Arts and crafts The museum has an outstanding collection of arts and crafts representing most of the great Islamic civilisations. You can see carved window shutters, wooden chests and gilded boxes, ceramic bowls, a 13th-century brass astrolabe, lacquer-on-leather bookbindings, calligraphic rolls and miniature paintings.

Carpets Hanging in the former Audience Hall of the palace are carpets from as far afield as Hungary, Persia and the Arab provinces of Spain. The earliest fragments date back to the 13th century and are of the kind that Marco Polo might have seen on his travels across Central Asia. Over time, the paired birds, animals and tree motifs favoured by the Seljuks give way to more stylised geometrical patterns. This transition is recorded in Western art of the period, so it is appropriate that the designs themselves are named after the artists in whose paintings the carpets appear: Bellini, Van Eyck, Holbein etc.

Ethnography The ethnography exhibition focuses on carpet-weaving as a domestic handicraft originating with the nomadic peoples of Anatolia. Besides learning about the sources of natural dyes, you can 'visit' a yurt, a goatskin black tent and other traditional dwellings.

HIGHLIGHTS

- Audience Hall
- 13th-century astrolabe
- Tile with leopard motif
- Engraved Selçuk drum
- Miniature Korans
- 'Holbein' carpet
- 'Bellini' carpet
- Yurt dwelling

INFORMATION

- ✠ M12
- ✉ Ibrahim Paşa Sarayı, At Meydanı 46, Sultanahmet
- ☎ 518 1805
- 🕐 Tue–Sun 10–5
- 🍴 Coffee-house (££)
- 🚇 Sultanahmet
- ♿ None
- 💰 Moderate
- ↔ At Meydanı (➤ 36), Yerebatan Sarayı (➤ 37), Sultanahmet Camii (➤ 38), Ayasofya Camii (➤ 40)

Ancient carpet exhibit

13

AT MEYDANı (HIPPODROME)

HIGHLIGHTS

- Kaiser Wilhelm fountain
- Egyptian Obelisk
- Serpent Column
- Column of Constantine Porphyrogenitus
- Brick and stone façade of İbrahim Paşa Sarayı (Museum of Turkish and Islamic Art; ➤ 35)
- Milion Taşı (First Milestone)
- View of Sultanahmet Mosque

INFORMATION

- M12
- At Meydanı, Sultanahmet
- Otel Alzer restaurant (£; ➤ 66)
- Sultanahmet
- None
- Free
- Sokullu Mehmet Paşa Camii (➤ 33), Türk ve İslâm Eserleri Müzesi (➤ 35), Yerebatan Sarayı (➤ 37), Sultanahmet Camii (➤ 38), Mozaik Müzesi (➤ 39), Ayasofya Camii (➤ 40), Topkapı Sarayı (➤ 42), Topkapı Sarayı Müzesi (➤ 43)

"In our view, the most remarkable survivor in the Hippodrome is the Egyptian Obelisk, commissioned by Pharaoh Thutmose III in the 16th century BC. The hieroglyph inscriptions are so sharply etched that at first sight the column looks like a modern reproduction."

At Meydanı Originally a racecourse for charioteers, the Hippodrome was laid out on the site of the present park by the Emperor Septimius Severus in AD 203 and enlarged by Constantine in the 4th century. The leading chariot teams, the Blues and the Greens, evolved into political factions and, in AD 532, rioted against the Emperor Justinian, provoking General Belisarius to storm the Hippodrome with the loss of 30,000 lives. The amphitheatre, which could hold 100,000 people, was destroyed during the Fourth Crusade and the Ottomans plundered the ruins for the Sultanahmet Mosque. From the 16th century the square was known as At Meydanı (Horses' Square), after a game resembling polo played here by the sultan's pages.

Monuments on the *spina* The racetrack was divided by a raised platform (*spina*), crowded with statues and monuments. Three of these survive, albeit in truncated form: the Egyptian Obelisk, brought to the city by the Emperor Theodosius in AD 390 (around the base are bas-reliefs showing episodes from the reign of Theodosius); the Serpent Column, imported by Constantine from the Temple of Apollo in Delphi (where it was raised to commemorate a 479 BC victory over the Persians); and the 10th-century Column of Constantine Porphyrogenitus.

Egyptian Obelisk

YEREBATAN SARAYı (BASILICA CISTERN)

"The Basilica Cistern can easily be missed for the obvious reason that it lies some 6m below ground. In our opinion, it is one of the most impressive sights in Istanbul. Stay for a coffee and soak up the atmosphere!"

Imperial reservoir The cistern dates from AD 532 and was built in the reign of the Emperor Justinian, primarily to supply water to the Grand Palace. Aqueducts carried the water from its source in the Belgrade Forest, about 19km away. After the Ottoman conquest the cistern fell into disuse, although attempts were made to repair it in the 18th and 19th centuries. It was only in 1987, however, after a great deal of patient restoration, that this magnificent building was finally opened to the public.

Exploring the cistern Water still drips from the ceiling of the imposing, brick-vaulted chamber, although the strategically placed spotlights and specially constructed gangways (not to mention the soothing classical music) make exploration easy. The main attraction – apart from the fish that thrive here in the remaining several inches of water – is the forest of pillars supporting the magnificent arched roof. Close inspection reveals that these columns are by no means uniform. Only about a third of the capitals are Corinthian, for example, while the patterning on one of the pillars resembles teardrops, on another peacock feathers. These inconsistencies suggest that they were removed from other sites and re-used here – presumably the builders reckoned no one would notice what went on underground! This might also account for the recent discovery of the two Medusa heads, one set upside-down, the other lying on its side.

DID YOU KNOW?

Basilica Cistern statistics
- 140m long, 70m wide
- Another section (40 x 30m) remains hidden
- Area of 9,800sq m
- Capacity of 80,000cu m
- 336 columns, each 12m high and 4.8m apart
- Outer walls 4m thick

INFORMATION

- ✚ L13
- ✉ Yerebatan Caddesi, Sultanahmet
- ☎ 522 1259
- ⊙ Daily 9–5:30
- 🍴 Café (£; ➤ 68)
- 🚇 Sultanahmet
- ♿ None
- 💷 Moderate
- ↔ Türk ve Islâm Eserleri Müzesi (➤ 35), At Meydanı (➤ 36), Sultanahmet Camii (➤ 38), Ayasofya Camii (➤ 40), Arkeoloji Müzesi (➤ 41), Topkapı Sarayı (➤ 42), Topkapı Sarayı Müzesi (➤ 43)
- ❓ Occasional concerts and plays

Medusa head

37

15

SULTANAHMET CAMII

HIGHLIGHTS

- Blue İznik tiles
- Six minarets
- Mausoleum of Sultan Ahmet I
- Inner courtyard
- Sultan's mansion
- Decorated wooden door and shutters
- Marble mimbar

"Better known to Western visitors as the 'Blue Mosque' because of the light that reflects brilliantly from the cobalt tiles in the prayer hall, this awesome building is particularly impressive when illuminated at night."

New mosque When Sultan Ahmet proposed building a new mosque in 1609, his advisers begged him to think again as the treasury was empty following a succession of failed military campaigns. But the sultan would have none of it and even insisted on digging the foundations himself. Sedefkar Mehmet Ağa, a pupil of Sinan, designed the mosque, which was completed in 1616. It immediately became the focus of religious activities in the city – every Friday the sultan's procession would make its way from Topkapı Palace after 16 muezzin had called the faithful to prayer from the six minarets.

INFORMATION

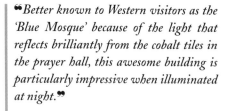

- ✚ M13
- ✉ Sultanahmet Meydanı, Sultanahmet
- ⏰ Daily, except during prayers
- 🍴 Cafés (££), restaurants (£££) near by
- 🚌 Sultanahmet
- ♿ None
- 💷 Free, gratuity
- ↔ Türk ve İslâm Eserleri Müzesi (➤ 35), At Meydanı (➤ 36), Yerebatan Sarayı (➤ 37), Mozaik Müzesi (➤ 39), Ayasofya Camii (➤ 40), Arkeoloji Müzesi (➤ 41), Topkapı Sarayı & Müzesi (➤ 42 & 43)

Külliye The inner courtyard comprises an ornamental fountain and a beautifully proportioned portico of 26 porphyry columns surmounted by 30 domes, while the view from above is of domes and semi-domes cascading from the mosque's summit in an apparently unbroken sequence.

Interior Inside, more than 20,000 İznik tiles decorate the walls and galleries. Delicately painted with floral and geometrical designs, they are the work of a master craftsman, Çinici Hasan Usta. The stencilling around the dome and the pillars is comparatively modern. Take a close look, too, at the wooden doors and window frames, with their inlay of ivory, tortoiseshell and mother-of-pearl, and at the beautiful carving on the mimbar and the sultan's loge.

MOZAIK MÜZESI

"One of the many remnants on view in the small Mosaic Museum shows an elephant strangling a lion with its trunk – a scene which may have been acted out in the Belgrade Forest more than 15 centuries ago."

The palace The mosaics were discovered during excavations in the Arasta Bazaar in the 1930s and 1950s. They are thought to date from the 6th century AD and belong to the first imperial palace. Begun in the reign of Constantine the Great (AD 324–37), the compound eventually stretched all the way from the Hippodrome to the sea walls, where there was a small private harbour known as the Buculeon (meaning 'Bull and Lion').

The museum Very little of the palace remains today apart from the ruined loggia at the entrance to the harbour and the superb mosaic friezes and pavements (the largest of which covers an area of 170sq m). These belonged to the peristyle (colonnade) of the Great Palace and would have been viewed by the emperors whenever they retired to their private apartments. Set in a background of white marble tesserae, the cubes of glass, stone and terracotta radiate colour while the action-packed scenes open a fascinating window onto everyday life in Byzantium. In one, a man falls from a donkey loaded with fruit; in another, a bear devours a young stag. There is a predilection for animal hunts featuring tigers, leopards, lions and elephants. But there are more domestic scenes too: birds perching on the branches of a cypress tree, or two children riding on a camel. The most splendid image is of Dionysus, the Greek god of wine and fruitfulness, his luxuriant beard wreathed in green acanthus leaves.

HIGHLIGHTS

- Marble window frames on palace ruins
- Broken pillars and capitals (in museum grounds)
- Mosaic fragments in Arasta Bazaar
- Mosaics: man falling from donkey; camel ride; Dionysus tiger hunt; bear and stag; fight between an elephant and a lion

INFORMATION

- ✚ M13
- ✉ Torun Sokağı, Sultanahmet
- ☎ 518 1205
- 🕐 Wed–Mon 9:30–5
- 🍴 Cafés (££), restaurants (£££) near by
- ♿ None
- ✋ Moderate; extra charge for photographs
- ↔ At Meydanı (➤ 36), Sultanahmet Camii (➤ 38), Ayasofya Camii (➤ 40)

Top: mosaic pavement depicting a fight between an elephant and a lion

17

AYASOFYA CAMII (HAGHIA SOPHIA)

HIGHLIGHTS

- Viking graffiti
- Gold mosaic ceiling in vestibule
- Shafts of light through 40 windows of dome
- Carved capitals
- Coloured marbles
- The Virgin and Christ flanked by Justinian and Constantine (mosaic in vestibule)
- Deisis mosaic in gallery
- 'Weeping column'

INFORMATION

✚ L13
✉ Ayasofya Meydanı, Sultanahmet
☎ 522 1750
🕐 Tue–Sun 9:30–5. Galleries: 9:30–11:30, 1:30–4:30
🍴 Cafés (£), restaurants (££) near by
🚇 Sultanahmet
♿ None
Ⓜ Moderate
↔ Türk ve İslâm Eserleri Müzesi (➤ 35), At Meydanı (➤ 36), Yerebatan Sarayı (➤ 37), Sultanahmet Camii (➤ 38), Mozaik Müzesi (➤ 39), Arkeoloji Müzesi (➤ 41), Topkapı Sarayı (➤ 42), Topkapı Sarayı Müzesi (➤ 43)
❓ Additional charge for photographs

"Despite the crumbling masonry and peeling mosaics, Ayasofya remains one of the world's great architectural master-pieces. While you are here, insert your finger into the 'weeping column' in the nave – it is said to have miraculous healing powers."

History Ayasofya (or Haghia Sophia), the Church of Divine Wisdom, was commissioned by the Emperor Justinian in AD 532. Despite its immense size – for a long time this was the largest religious building in the world – Ayasofya was completed in just five years by two outstanding architects, Anthemius of Tralles and Isidore of Miletus. Earthquakes nearly destroyed the building shortly afterwards, but despite this and many other vicissitudes, Ayasofya remained the most important church in Christendom for nearly a thousand years. When, in 1453, Constantinople fell to the Turks, Sultan Mehmet II decreed that the basilica should become a mosque. Since 1934 it has been the Ayasofya Museum.

Mosaics The walls and pillars of the basilica are of patterned and decorated marbles, brought to Constantinople from all over the known world: white marble from the Marmara, purple porphyry from Egypt, verd antique from Thessaly and yellow marble from North Africa. But the chief glory of Ayasofya is its mosaics. There were originally more than 4 acres of gold tesserae, and although a great deal has since disappeared you can still see some stunning figurative mosaics, dating from the 9th to 13th centuries, in the Vestibule of the Warriors (narthex) and the galleries. There are portraits of emperors and an incomplete but arresting Deisis (Christ flanked by the Virgin Mary and John the Baptist).

ARKEOLOJI MÜZESI

We were not surprised when the exemplary Archaeological Museum won the Council of Europe Award in 1993. The star attraction, in our view, is the magnificent Alexander sarcophagus, carved with hunting and battle scenes of astonishing savagery and intensity.

Archaeological Museum Built to house the sarcophagi of the ancient Phoenician kings recovered by the archaeologist Osman Hamdi Bey in 1887, the museum also boasts a superb collection of classical sculptures. They include some astonishingly lifelike busts of the Roman emperors, funerary stelae with moving valedictory scenes, and a number of remarkably well-preserved statues. The new wing hosts a fascinating exhibition on the history of Istanbul and the neighbouring regions. Here you will find fragments of artwork preserved from lost Byzantine churches and a section of the defensive chain that hung across the Golden Horn in the 15th century.

Museum of the Ancient Orient A pair of 14th-century BC Hittite lions guard the entrance to this museum, which contains a fabulous collection of ancient art and artefacts. One of the most significant is a tablet containing the world's oldest peace accord, the Treaty of Kadesh, made in 1269 BC between Pharaoah Rameses II and the Hittite King Muvatellish. You can also see the world's oldest law code, dictated by the Assyrian King Hammurabi in 1740 BC. But it is the reliefs that take the breath away: there are sections from the glazed-tile walls which once formed the glorious Processional Way into Babylon and some vivid narrative friezes – look on in awe as the charioteers of Assyria rumble inexorably into battle.

HIGHLIGHTS

- Alexander's sarcophagus
- Sarcophagus of the Mourning Women
- Lycian Sarcophagus
- Statue of Oceanus
- Bust of Emperor Augustus
- Phrygian alabaster perfume bottle in the shape of a goddess
- Gold earrings from Bronze Age Troy
- Treaty of Kadesh
- Relief of Hittite King Urpalla with the god of vegetation

INFORMATION

- ✚ L13
- ✉ Sarayıçi Osman Hamdi Yokşu, Gülhane Parkı, Eminönü
- ☎ 520 7740
- 🕐 Tue–Sun 9:30–5
- 🍴 Garden café (£; ➤ 68)
- 🚇 Gülhane
- 🚌 Few
- ♿ Moderate
- ↔ Yerebatan Sarayı (➤ 37), Sultanahmet Camii (➤ 38), Ayasofya Camii (➤ 40), Topkapı Sarayı (➤ 42), Topkapı Sarayı Müzesi (➤ 43)

TOPKAPI SARAYI

HIGHLIGHTS

- Gate of the White Eunuchs
- Divan
- Audience Hall
- Sultan's throne
- Baghdad Pavilion
- Imperial Hall
- Murat III's bedroom
- Sultan's bath
- Ahmet III's dining-room
- 'Eye of the Sultan' grille (Divan)

INFORMATION

✚ L13
✉ Topkapı, Sultanahmet
☎ 512 0480
🕐 Wed–Mon 9:30–5. Harem: 10–4
🍴 Café (££), Konyalı restaurant (££; ➤ 62)
🚇 Gülhane
♿ None
💷 Moderate; separate charge for Harem
🔄 At Meydanı (➤ 36), Yerebatan Sarayı (➤ 37), Sultanahmet Camii (➤ 38), Ayasofya Camii (➤ 40), Arkeoloji Müzesi (➤ 41), Topkapı Sarayı Müzesi (➤ 43)
❓ 30-minute guided tour of the Harem must be booked in advance to avoid long queues

“When visiting the Topkapı Palace, don't miss the Fourth Courtyard – the terraces, pavilions and rose gardens are a treat, and there are unmatched views of the Sea of Marmara and the Bosphorus.”

The palace From 1461, when Mehmet II ordered its construction, until 1856, when Abdülhamid left for Dolmabahçe (➤ 45), Topkapı was both the private residence of the sultans and their families and the administrative centre of the Ottoman Empire. The most important building in the Second Courtyard is the Divan (Imperial Council Chamber), where the sultan's advisers met to discuss matters of state four days a week. Restored to its 16th-century appearance, the council chamber still contains the *divan*, or couch, where the grand vizier presided over meetings while the sultan kept a watchful eye through the grille in the wall above. From the canopied throne the sultan would receive foreign ambassadors and other dignitaries with elaborate protocol and ceremony.

The Harem The private quarters of the sultan and his family, the Harem, was a palace within a palace, with its own baths, hospital and kitchens, and at least 300 rooms lost in a labyrinth of corridors and courtyards. There were two separate domains: that of the *valide sultan* (queen mother); and the *selamlık*, the preserve of the sultan himself. Visitors are shown the Imperial Hall, where dancers and musicians entertained the sultan and his concubines; the suite of marble-clad bathrooms; Murat III's bedroom, complete with fountain and stained-glass windows; and the dining-room of Ahmet III, gorgeously decorated with fruit and floral motifs.

20

TOPKAPI SARAYI MÜZESI

"Why is it that the sultans were so keen to acquire vast quantities of celadon porcelain, as seen here at the Topkapı Palace Museum? Might it have had anything to do with the rumour that celadon could expose poisoned food?"

Collections of the Second Courtyard The palace kitchens, with their distinctive domes and tall chimneys, are now home to one of the world's finest collections of Chinese porcelain, celadon and silverware – some items date back to the 10th century. Original pieces of kitchen equipment, including giant *kazans* (cauldrons), ladles, platters and copper dishes, are on display at the far end of the building. Across the courtyard in the Inner Treasury is a superb collection of arms and armour, including many items belonging to the sultans themselves. You can see the sword of Mehmet the Conqueror, the armour of Selim the Grim's horse and a bow made by Bayezid II.

Collections of the Third Courtyard A dazzling array of costumes belonging to the sultans and crown princes, including kaftans of satin, silk and velvet brocade, embroidered jackets, quilted turbans, scarves and slippers is on show in the Pages' Quarters, while in the Treasury you can see jewellery belonging to the imperial family and the spoils of war from various military campaigns. The prize exhibit here is the famous emerald-studded Topkapı dagger. There is also an exquisite collection of Turkish and Persian miniatures, some dating from the 16th century. In the Pavilion of the Holy Mantle you can see sacred relics of the Prophet Muhammad, including the mantle itself, hairs from the Prophet's beard, his footprint and one of his teeth.

HIGHLIGHTS

- Chinese porcelain, celadon and silver
- Original kitchen equipment
- Sword of Mehmet the Conqueror
- Armour of Selim the Grim's horse
- Costumes of sultans
- Imperial jewellery
- Topkapı dagger
- Spoonmaker's Diamond
- Turkish and Persian miniatures
- Relics of the Prophet Muhammad

INFORMATION

- L13
- Topkapı, Sultanahmet
- 512 0480
- Wed–Mon 9:30–5. Harem: 10–4
- Café (££), restaurant (£££)
- Gülhane
- None
- Moderate
- At Meydanı (➤ 36), Yerebatan Sarayı (➤ 37), Sultanahmet Camii (➤ 38), Ayasofya Camii (➤ 40), Arkeoloji Müzesi (➤ 41), Topkapı Sarayı (➤ 42)

Mehmet the Conqueror's sword

21

BOĞAZIÇI

HIGHLIGHTS

- Rumeli Hisarı (➤ 54)
- Ortaköy Camii (➤ 51)
- Dolmabahçe Sarayı (➤ 45)
- Küçüksu Kasrı (➤ 54)
- Beylerbeyi Sarayı (➤ 48)
- Wooden mansions (yalıs)
- Two bridges
- Sarıyer fish market and restaurants
- Genoese castle at Anadolu Kavağı (➤ 58)
- Kanlıca yoghurt

INFORMATION

- K14/15–C19/20 and beyond
- By main landing stages
- Beşiktaş, Kanlıca, Yeniköy, Sarıyer, Anadolu Kavağı and many others
- None
- Cheap – Turkish Maritime Lines ferry (➤ 56) Bosphorus round trip is half price at weekends
- Dolmabahçe Sarayı (➤ 45), Yıldız Parkı (➤ 46), Sadberk Hanım Müzesi (➤ 47), Beylerbeyi Sarayı (➤ 48)

Top: wooden mansions (yalıs) along the shoreline

❝*One of the most pleasurable and unforgettable experiences in Istanbul is to sail out onto the Bosphorus. You will be entranced by vistas of sun-bleached fishing villages, crumbling medieval fortresses, sumptuous Ottoman palaces and shuttered* yalıs.**❞**

Ford of the ox The Bosphorus is a narrow stretch of water about 30km long which threads its way from the Sea of Marmara to the Black Sea, forming a natural barrier between Europe and Asia. Bosphorus means 'ford of the ox' and derives from the Greek myth of Io. While being hotly pursued by Hera, wife of Zeus, Io is turned into an ox and in that guise escapes across the strait. Today, there is no need to swim as the Bosphorus is spanned by two road bridges.

Ports of call The cheapest way to see the Bosphorus is to take the ferry – Turkish Maritime Lines ferries sail twice daily from Eminönü (➤ 56). There are several stops *en route*, offering a variety of attractions: Kanlıca is famous for its yoghurt, served with jam, sugar or ice-cream in the square behind the pier. You will come to know Yeniköy by the splendid art nouveau mansions that line the waterfront – scarcely a passenger leaves without discovering their ideal home here. You can see Sarıyer's colourful fishing fleet unload its catch at the quayside market, or go swimming in the Black Sea at Kilyos (only a short bus ride away). Before returning to Istanbul, the ferry ties up for an hour in the secluded harbour of Anadolu Kavağı, giving you enough time to climb the hill to the Genoese castle (➤ 58), or to stop for lunch in one of the cheap waterfront restaurants. If you return on the later ferry there's the added bonus of a beautiful sunset as you approach the city – a photographer's dream.

DOLMABAHÇE SARAYI

" *While the taste of the builders of Dolmabahçe Palace might be subject to doubt, its entertainment value lies in the sheer extravagance of the interiors – a relentless accumulation of ostentatious luxury and rococo excess.* **"**

A new palace By far the most sumptuous of the sultans' palaces, Dolmabahçe stands on the site of a reclaimed harbour – the Turkish word means 'filled-in garden'. It was commissioned by Sultan Abdülmecit from the architects Karabet Balyan and his son, Nikoğos, in 1843, and the royal entourage moved here from Topkapı 13 years later. So much of the state's revenues were thrown at this *folie de grandeur* that it contributed in part to the bankrupting of the Ottoman treasury in 1881. The first President of the Republic, Mustafa Kemal Atatürk, returned to Dolmabahçe in 1927, rechristening it the Palace of the Nation, and died here on 10 November 1938.

Interiors The layout of the palace preserves the traditional division between *selamlık* (state rooms) and *harem* (private apartments). Separating the two is the largest throne room in the world, its *trompe-l'oeil* ceiling supported by 56 Corinthian columns. It was here that the first Ottoman parliament was convened in 1877. Other highlights include the magnificent formal staircase, with a balustrade of Baccarat crystal; the Hünkâr Hamamı (Sultan's Bathroom), with walls of alabaster specially imported from Egypt; and the dazzling Mavi Salon. The décor is almost exclusively Western, after a style the French novelist, Théophile Gautier, described ironically as 'Louis XIV *orientalisé*'. The furniture was supplied by William Gibbs Rogers of London and Sechan of Paris.

HIGHLIGHTS

- 248m marble façade
- Throne Room
- Bed of Sultan Abdülaziz
- Ceremonial crystal staircase
- Sultan's private bathroom
- Atatürk's bedroom
- Clock stopped at 09:05 (exact time of Atatürk's death)

INFORMATION

- ⊞ G15
- ✉ Dolmabahçe Caddesi, Beşiktaş
- ☎ 258 5544
- ◷ Tue–Wed, Fri–Sun 9–6
- ⛴ Beşiktaş Vapur İskelesi
- ♿ None
- 💲 Moderate
- ↔ Boğaziçi (➤ 44), Yıldız Parkı (➤ 46)
- ❓ Group admission with tour guide

The palace ballroom

23

YILDIZ PARKI

HIGHLIGHTS

Palace
- Tiyatro
- Harem Gate
- Yaveran Dairesi
- Palace fountains
- Hamidiye Camii
- Carved table with inlaid porcelain panels (in Palace Museum)
- Ornamental halter for sacrificial ram (in Silahhane)

Park
- Şale Köşkü
- Yıldız Porcelain Factory (➤ 75)

INFORMATION

- ✚ E/F16/17
- ✉ Palace: Barbaros Bulvarı, Çırağan. Park: Yıldız Caddesi and Çırağan Caddesi, Çırağan
- ☎ 258 3080
- 🕐 Museums: Wed–Sun 9:30–4:30. Şale Köşkü: Oct–Feb Tue–Wed, Fri–Sun 9:30–4. Mar–Sep Tue–Wed, Fri–Sun 9:30–5. Park: daily 8:30–5:30
- 🍴 Cafés (£), restaurants (£££)
- 🚇 Beşiktaş
- ♿ None
- 💰 Cheap
- ↔ Boğaziçi (➤ 44), Dolmabahçe Sarayı (➤ 45)

"The last of the great Ottoman palaces, Yıldız Sarayı, is mainly popular for its stunning grounds, Yıldız Park, a favourite with Istanbul's courting couples. It is likely to become even more popular with tourists as the splendid buildings are once again opened to the public."

Hilltop palace Abdülhamid II commissioned the hilltop palace in 1876 because it was more secure from attack than Dolmabahçe (➤ 45).

Museums There are currently two museums within the palace open to the public: the Marangozhane (Palace Museum) and, next door, the Belediye Şehir Müzesi (City Museum). Highly entertaining exhibits display a whole range of Ottoman treasures, from hand-painted Yıldız porcelain and elegant 19th-century furniture to silver dessert sets, copper incense burners, prayer beads, glass walking sticks, calligraphic paintings, a janissary's chin-strap and an ornamental halter for a sacrificial ram! Ask at the desk for someone to show you inside the exquisite theatre in the courtyard behind the Harem Gate, where an Italian company, the Arturo Stravolo Players, performed nightly for the harem and guests of the sultan.

Yıldız Parkı Yıldız Palace stands in a magnificent 50-hectare park, where the air is heavy with the scent of orange blossom. The star attraction is the Şale Köşkü, a miniature palace built for the state visit of Kaiser Wilhelm II of Germany in 1889 (open to the public). A map by the park gate will point you in the direction of some of the other attractions, including several elegant mansions, now converted to tearooms, and the red-brick Yıldız Porcelain Factory (➤ 75).

SADBERK HANIM MÜZESI

" *Do you know what a* **taka-tuka** *bowl is? Or a* **bindalli***? Would you know what to do at a henna party or who to expect on Trotter Day? All is revealed in the fascinating exhibition on Turkish marriage customs in the Sadberk Hanım Museum.* **"**

Archaeological finds The oldest exhibit is a mother goddess, made from clay and dating from about 5000 BC. Subsequently, Anatolia was invaded by wave after wave of ancient peoples, beginning with the Hittites and Assyrian trading colonists in around 2000 BC, and ending only with the Roman conquest of Asia Minor in 133 BC. Each of these societies left an indelible mark on Anatolian civilisation, as you can see from the fabulous displays of painted pots and drinking vessels, oil lamps, ornaments and jewellery, gold leaf, bronze busts, terracotta figurines, perfume flasks, glass jars, coins and votive offerings. Moving through the displays, you can appreciate the advances in technical mastery as well as the growing aesthetic awareness and sense of accomplishment.

Ethnography The ethnographical exhibit is just as rewarding. The sheer wealth and variety of chased and inlaid metalwork created by generations of Seljuk, Mamluk and Ottoman craftsmen from the 8th to the 18th centuries is to be wondered at, as is the consummate artistry of the creators of İznik and Kütahya ceramics. If these were the men's trades, then embroidery – using linen, velvet, silk and gold thread – was the women's domain. You can see exquisitely woven bedspreads, sashes, towels, napkins, triple-skirted dresses and wedding gowns.

HIGHLIGHTS

- Neolithic clay goddess
- Bronze Age gold-mounted marble mace
- Assyrian cuneiform tablet
- Corinthian perfume flasks
- Bronze child's head
- Gold ring with garnet and turquoise
- Roman glass jug with handle
- Bronze ewer from Khoransan
- İznik polychrome dish
- Yellow dress with triple-skirt

Late 16th-century ceramic İznik tankard

INFORMATION

- Off map at C19
- Piyası Caddesi 27–9, Sarıyer
- 242 3813
- Oct–Mar Thu–Tue 10–5. Apr–Sep Thu–Tue 10:30–6
- Restaurants (££) on Piyasa Caddesi
- Sarıyer İskelesi
- None
- Moderate
- Boğaziçi (▶ 44)
- Discount on group visits and for students

47

25

BEYLERBEYI SARAYI

"You arrive at Beylerbeyi Palace to the beguiling sounds of oriental music, transmitted through speakers concealed among the magnolias of the beautiful terrace garden. Before the guided tour begins, stop for a moment to admire the wonderful views across the Bosphorus to Ortaköy."

French empress This attractive summer palace was built for Sultan Abdülaziz in 1861 by Sarkis Balyan, brother of the architect of Dolmabahçe (➤ 45). The deposed Sultan Abdülhamid II also lived here for the six years before his death in 1918. But the most celebrated occupant was Empress Eugénie of France, wife of Napoleon III, who stayed here in 1869 *en route* to opening the Suez Canal. Abdülaziz is said to have become infatuated with her after attending the Paris exhibition two years earlier, and went to immense trouble to make her visit an enjoyable one. Eugénie never forgot her stay and returned to Beylerbeyi in 1910 at the ripe old age of 85.

The palace Comprising just 24 rooms and six salons, divided into the traditional *selamlık* and *harem*, Beylerbeyi is more modest, though no less luxurious than Dolmabahçe. To keep the apartments cool in summer, all the floors were covered with rush mats and a recessed marble pool and fountain were built into the floor of the Pool Salon – one of the most impressive rooms in the palace. Abdülaziz was a keen sailor – nautical scenes predominate in the paintings at Belerbeyi, and in the Admiral's Sitting Room all the furniture is ingeniously carved with rope motifs. Visitors are also shown Empress Eugénie's suite with its specially Westernised bathroom, the Sultan's prayer room and the 2m-long bed reinforced to accommodate his enormous frame – he was a formidable wrestler!

Top: harem room

ISTANBUL's
best

MOSQUES & CHURCHES

Know your mosques

There are three features common to all mosques:

● the minaret, a tall, tapered tower with balconies used by the muezzin to summon the faithful to prayer;

● the mihrab, a highly decorated marble niche, which points worshippers in the direction of Mecca; and

● the mimbar, an elaborate staircase leading to a hooded pulpit from which the imam preaches on festival days.

Fatih Camii minarets

AYA IRINI (CHURCH OF DIVINE PEACE)
This sturdy brick church is one of the oldest religious buildings in Istanbul. It was commissioned by Emperor Justinian in AD 537, about the same time as Ayasofya (➤ 40). Of the once-lavish interior decoration, only a stunning mosaic of Christ on the Cross survives.
🚹 L13 ⊠ First Courtyard, Topkapı Sarayı 🍴 Cafés (££) near by 🚇 Gülhane 🚻 Few 🎵 Closed except for concerts (➤ 78)

DOLMABAHÇE CAMII
Occupying a superb site overlooking the Bosphorus, this mosque (completed in 1855) was built by the architect Sarkis Balyan for the mother of Sultan Abdülmecit. Look out for the sultan's two-storey private pew.
🚹 G14 ⊠ Meclisi Mebusan Caddesi 🕐 Hours of prayer 🚢 Kabataş İskelesi 🚻 None 🎵 Free

FATIH CAMII
Named after the conqueror of Constantinople, Sultan Fatih Mehmet, this important mosque complex actually dates from 1767 – its predecessor (built in 1463–70) was completely destroyed in an earthquake. You can see Fatih's tomb in front of the mihrab wall.
🚹 K10 ⊠ Fevzi Paşa Caddesi, Fatih 🕐 Hours of prayer 🍴 Cafés (£), restaurants (££) near by 🚻 None 🎵 Free

IMRAHOR CAMII (ST JOHN OF STUDION)
Now reduced to a haunting ruin, this former monastery church dates from AD 463 and is named after the Roman consul, Studius. Although much of the sumptuous decoration has sadly disappeared, the entrance, with its four marble Corinthian columns, frieze and cornice, are still impressive.
🚹 N8 ⊠ İmam Asır Sokağı, İmrahor İlyas Bey Caddesi, Fatih 🕐 Daily 🍴 Cafés (£) near by 🚇 Yedikule 🚻 None 🎵 Free, gratuity

KALENDERHANE CAMII

The 12th-century Byzantine Church of Theotokos Kiriotissa (Our Lady Mother of God) has been painstakingly restored by archaeologists. Although visiting is restricted, it is worth trying to get inside to see the surviving marble decoration and mosaic fragments, including the Theotokos Kiriotissa herself and reputedly the earliest fresco depiction of St Francis of Assisi.

➕ L11 ⊠ 16 Mart Şehitleri Caddesi, Eminönü 🕐 Hours of prayer
🍴 Cafés (£) in nearby streets
♿ None 💵 Free, gratuity

Mesih Mehmet Paşa Camii, on Akşemsettin Caddesi in Fatih, burial place of the eunuch and notoriously cruel governor of Egypt, Mesih Mehmet

NURUOSMANIYE CAMII

Casting a shadow across the Nuruosmaniye Gate of the Covered Bazaar is the mosque that gives it its name, possibly the finest example of Ottoman baroque architecture in Istanbul. It was completed in 1755 in the reign of Osman III.

➕ L12 ⊠ Nuruosmaniye Caddesi, Çemberlitaş 🕐 Hours of prayer
🍴 Cafés (£) 🚇 Çemberlitaş ♿ None 💵 Free

ORTAKÖY CAMII

This pearl of a mosque, its dome and twin minarets reflected in the waters of the Bosphorus, was designed by Nikoğos Balyan in 1854 for Sultan Abdülmecit. It is unusual for its ornate *beaux-arts* decoration.

➕ F17 ⊠ Eski Vapur İskelesi Sokak, Ortaköy 🕐 Hours of prayer 🍴 Cafés (£) and restaurants (££) on quay
🚇 Ortaköy Vapur İskelesi ♿ None 💵 Free

ŞEHZADE CAMII

The 'Prince's Mosque' was built in the 1540s to commemorate Mehmet, son of Süleyman the Magnificent, who died of smallpox aged 21. It was the architect Sinan's first major commission and has an austere simplicity missing from his later works. The tiling in Mehmet's mausoleum at the side of the mosque is particularly beautiful, creating a paradise garden in green, blue and yellow.

➕ L11 ⊠ Şehzadebaşı Caddesi, Şehzadebaşı 🕐 Hours of prayer ♿ None 💵 Free

YENI CAMII

This imposing mosque dominates the approaches to the Galata Bridge. It was commissioned towards the end of the 16th century but not completed until 1663. The two-storey building on the forecourt is the sultan's 'private pew', actually a suite of luxuriously appointed rooms with sea views and a private toilet.

➕ K12 ⊠ Yeni Cami Caddesi, Eminönü 🕐 Hours of prayer 🍴 Cafés (£) near by 🚇 Eminönü ♿ None
💵 Free

Mosque etiquette

Muslims welcome visitors, but it is respectful to observe the following customs:

● women should always cover their heads and wear modest clothing;

● men should wear trousers rather than shorts, and shirts not vests;

● men and women should remove their shoes as they step onto the carpet at the entrance to the mosque; and

● once inside, visitors should confine themselves to the perimeter of the prayer hall and show consideration to worshippers.

51

STREETS

See Top 25 Sights for
AT MEYDANI (HIPPODROME) ➤ 36
KAPALI ÇARŞI (COVERED BAZAAR) ➤ 30

Old tram system in Beyoğlu

Relocation

Foreign diplomats began moving from their cramped houses in Galata to the vineyards and open spaces of the rue de Pera before the Ottoman conquest. From the 16th to the 18th centuries, the ambassadors of all the major powers built palatial residences for themselves on either side of the street (now İstiklâl Caddesi), which became the focus of the various 'Nations' or merchant communities. When the ambassadors moved to Ankara in the 1920s, their Istanbul premises were relegated to the status of consulate.

DIVAN YOLU

Back in the reign of Constantine the Great this was the main street of Byzantium, known as the Mese (Middle Way). Centuries later it became Divan Yolu (Road of the Divan Council), the traditional Ottoman processional route from the city to Topkapı Palace. Today, this narrow, tree-lined thoroughfare is the preserve of bureaux de change offices, travel agents, late-night bars and cheap neighbourhood restaurants.

➕ L12 ✉ Divan Yolu, Sultanahmet 🍴 Cafés (£) and restaurants (££) 🚊 Sultanahmet, Çemberlitaş

GALATA KULESI SOKAĞI

A flight of stone steps leads up to this steep and narrow street, typical of the Galata neighbourhood. The Genoese, who built the nearby Galata Tower (➤ 58), were also responsible for the 15th-century Dominican church of Ss Peter and Paul.

➕ J12 ✉ Galata Kulesi Sokağı, Galata

İSTIKLÂL CADDESİ

İstiklâl Caddesi (Independence Avenue) is Istanbul's most famous shopping street and the focus of evening entertainment. Known in the 19th century as the Grand rue de Pera, this was the heart of the city's European quarter and was where most of the foreign embassies were located (many are still here today). A restored 19th-century tram runs the entire length of the pedestrianised street (1.2km).

➕ J12–H13 ✉ İstiklâl Caddesi, Beyoğlu 🍴 Cafés (£), restaurants (££) 🚊 Tünel 🚊 İstiklâl Caddesi 🚫 None 🎫 Free

MAHMUTPAŞA YOKUŞU

Located between the Spice and the Covered bazaars, this street is packed with local people on the lookout for cheap clothes, bags and shoes. At the bottom of the street are the Mahmutpaşa Baths, dating from 1476 and also now converted into shops.

➕ L12 ✉ Mahmutpaşa Yokuşu, Mahmutpaşa 🍴 Cafés (£)

SOĞUKÇEŞME SOKAK

Overlooking the walls of Topkapı Palace, this ancient street with its attractive wooden houses and cobbled pavements is typical of Sultanahmet. Some of the houses have been restored as the Ayasofya Pensions (➤ 85), while the Roman cistern is now a restaurant.

➕ L13 ✉ Soğukçeşme Sokak, Sultanahmet 🍴 Sarnıç Restaurant (££; ➤ 62) 🚊 Gülhane

Free Attractions

See Top 25 Sights for

BEŞIKTAŞ PROMENADE

You can stop to watch the passengers disembarking at the elegant, art nouveau jetty, join the promenaders strolling by the Bosphorus or linger over coffee at one of the cafés.

➕ G15 ⊠ Beşiktaş Vapur İskelesi ⏰ Daily 🍴 Cafés (£) and restaurants (££) 🚢 Beşiktaş ♿ None

BÜYÜKADA

A cheap ferry ride will take you to this beautiful island, where you can enjoy a walk along the promenade and through the old streets of the town. Alternatively, you could spend the afternoon sunbathing on one of the island's beaches or enjoy a picnic in the shady pine forests that cover its southern hills.

➕ Off map ⊠ Büyükada, Princes' Islands ⏰ Daily 🍴 Cafés (£), restaurants (££) 🚢 Büyükada ♿ None

GÜLHANE PARK

This wooded park in the heart of Sultanahmet was created from the old rose garden of Topkapı Palace. Apart from the views of the Bosphorus and the statue of Atatürk, you can admire the Alay Köşkü (Review Pavilion) built into the wall by the main gate. From the rooms here the sultan could observe the goings on in the park while keeping an eye on the office of his grand vizier near by.

➕ L13 ⊠ Alemdar Caddesi ⏰ Daily 🍴 Cafés 🚇 Gülhane ♿ None

VALENS AQUEDUCT

This impressive double-arched aqueduct was built in the 4th century AD by Emperor Valens to carry water across the valley between the fourth and the third hills (Fatih to Beyazıt). About 625m of the original 1km remain and can be seen to best advantage from the grounds of the Şehzade Camii.

➕ K11 ⊠ Şehzadebaşı Caddesi ⏰ Daily ♿ None

Sinan the architect

Sinan, the chief architect of Süleyman the Magnificent and his successors, Selim II and Murad III, was born in Kayseri, Anatolia, around 1500. He trained as an engineer and served in numerous military campaigns before turning to architecture. About half of the 477 buildings he designed before his death in 1588 are in Istanbul. They include mosques, palaces, mausoleums, bridges, hospitals, aqueducts and baths.

The imposing two-tier arches of the Valens Aqueduct

ISTANBUL'S BEST

PALACES & CASTLES

See Top 25 Sights for
BEYLERBEYI SARAYI ➤ 48
DOLMABAHÇE SARAYI ➤ 45
TEKFUR SARAYI ➤ 24
TOPKAPI SARAYI ➤ 42
YEDIKULE CASTLE ➤ 24
YILDIZ SARAYI ➤ 46

Royal execution

The traditional death meted out to a member of the imperial family was strangulation by bow string so that no royal blood would be shed. Among those to suffer this terrible fate was the 17-year-old Sultan Osman II. He died in 1622 in the dank dungeons of Yedikule Castle.

ANADOLU HISARI

Deservedly known in Turkish as 'the Beautiful One', this small castle was begun in about 1390 by Sultan Bayezid I. The barbican and towers were added by Mehmet II just before the city's conquest in 1453.
🚫 Off map at C20 ✉ Körfez Caddesi ☎ (216) 263 5305
🕐 Daily 🍴 Café (£) near by 🚢 Anadolu Hisarı Vapur İskelesi 🚻 None 🎟 Cheap

ANADOLU KAVAĞI ➤ 58

ÇIRAĞAN PALACE

This stately waterfront palace was commissioned by Sultan Abdülaziz and completed in 1874. His successor, Murat V, was confined here for more than 30 years after he was deposed in 1876. The palace was destroyed by fire in 1910 and has only recently been restored and reopened as a luxury hotel.
🚫 G16 ✉ Çırağan Caddesi 84, Beşiktaş ☎ 258 3377
🕐 To hotel visitors and guests 🍴 Cafés and restaurants (£££) 🚢 Beşiktaş Vapur İskelesi 🚻 Few 🎟 Free

KÜÇÜKSU KASRI

This pleasing pseudo-baroque palace was built for Sultan Abdülmecit by Nikoğos Balyan in 1856–7. You can make the small tour of the palace or take a picnic in the meadows. The wooded promenade in front of the palace leads to the delightful Küçüksu Fountain, built for Sultan Selim III in 1806.
🚫 Off map at C20 ✉ Anadolu Hisarı, Küçüksu Caddesi 🕐 Tue–Wed, Fri–Sun 9–4 🚢 Anadolu Hisarı İskelesi 🚻 None 🎟 Moderate

Rumeli Hisarı fortress, medieval guardian of the Bosphorus

RUMELI HISARI

This superb fortress was built in 1452 by Mehmet II. You can explore the walls and garden terraces, and, in the summer months, attend a concert or play here.
🚫 Off map at C19 ✉ Bebek-Rumeli Hisarı Caddesi ☎ 263 5305 🕐 Tue–Sun 9:30–5 🚢 Rumeli Hisarı Vapur İskelesi 🚻 None 🎟 Cheap

MUSEUMS

CALLIGRAPHY MUSEUM
The only museum in the world devoted to this art form. The displays include a reconstruction of a calligraphy workshop.
🏛 L12 ⊠ Beyazıt Meydanı, Beyazıt ☎ 527 5851
🕐 Tue–Sat 9–4 🍴 Cafés (£) near by 🚇 Beyazıt
♿ None 💲 Cheap

CARPET AND KILIM MUSEUM
This fabulous collection of ancient kilims and carpets is housed within the precincts of the Blue Mosque in the Hünkâr Kasrı, a mansion belonging to the sultans.
🏛 M13 ⊠ Sultanahmet Camii, Sultanahmet ☎ 518 1330 🕐 Tue–Sat 9–12, 1–4 🍴 Cafés and restaurants (££) near by 🚇 Sultanahmet ♿ None 💲 Free

MILITARY MUSEUM
Impressive displays of Ottoman and Turkish military uniforms, weapons, battle standards and magnificent campaign tents. Musicians in the guise of a Janissary band perform for visitors in season 3–4PM.
🏛 F14 ⊠ Valikonağı Caddesi, Harbiye ☎ 240 6255
🕐 Wed–Sun 9–5 🍴 Cafés (££), restaurants (£££) near by ♿ None 💲 Moderate

NAVAL MUSEUM
This museum houses sailors' uniforms, model ships, paintings of naval engagements, maps and engravings – everything nautical in fact. The highlights are the infamous *Barbarossa* and the splendid *caiques*, or barges, used to ferry sultans. Be sure to visit both sections of the museum.
🏛 G15 ⊠ Cezayir Caddesi, Beşiktaş ☎ 261 0040
🕐 Wed–Sun 9:30–5 🍴 Cafés (£) near by ⛴ Beşiktaş Vapur İskelesi ♿ None 💲 Moderate

RAHMI M KOÇ INDUSTRIAL MUSEUM
A wonderful museum of things industrial, from tools and machines dating back to the Industrial Revolution to scale models of ships, steam engines and automobiles, plus a hand-operated train set.
🏛 G10 ⊠ Hasköy Caddesi 27, Sütlüce (Golden Horn)
☎ 256 7153 🕐 Tue–Sun 10–5 🍴 Café du Levant (££)
⛴ Hasköy Vapur İskesi ♿ None 💲 Moderate

Inspiration
The *mehter* (musical band) of the Janissaries, the sultans' imperial guard, marched before the army and accompanied the soldiers into battle. The kettledrums, which played no small part in arousing their aggressive instincts, eventually found their way into the Western orchestra via Glück's 18th-century opera *Iphigénie en Tauride*.

Artillery and cannon at the Naval Museum

BOAT JOURNEYS

Bosphorus tour boat

Waiter service

Light refreshments are available on most of the city's ferries from the snack bar in the saloon. Or you can sit on deck and wait to be served by the business-like, white-jacketed waiters who pop up every five minutes or so with trays of tea, coffee, fruit juices and yoghurt. They tend to add on a small commission for the convenience.

BOSPHORUS ROUND TRIPS

There are several ways to see the Bosphorus, but the cheapest option is to take the round trip which leaves twice daily from Eminönü jetty number 3 (to the right of the Galata Bridge).

✚ K12 ✉ Eminönü İskelesi 3, Eminönü ☎ 522 0045 ⏲ Daily 10:35 and 1:35. Extra boats at weekends in the summer 🍴 Snack bar on board 🚌 Eminönü ♿ None 🖐 Cheap (half price at weekends)

EYÜP AND GOLDEN HORN

Small ferries ply up and down Istanbul's natural harbour, the Golden Horn, from Eminönü jetty number 4.

✚ K12 ✉ Eminönü İskelesi 4, Eminönü ☎ 528 5644 ⏲ Times displayed at jetty 🚌 Eminönü ♿ None 🖐 Cheap

HAREM

A car ferry makes regular trips to Harem on the Asian side (useful for Haydarpaşa railway station), departing from Sirkeci between the Kadıköy and Adalar jetties.

✚ K13 ✉ Araba Vapur İskelesi, Sirkeci ☎ 522 0055 ⏲ Times displayed at jetty 🍴 Snack bar 🚌 Eminönü ♿ None 🖐 Cheap

KADIKÖY

The ferries from jetty number 1 at Eminönü take foot passengers to this busy shopping area on the Asian side.

✚ K12 ✉ Eminönü İskelesi 1, Eminönü ☎ 526 1503 ⏲ Times displayed at jetty 🍴 Snack bar 🚌 Eminönü ♿ None 🖐 Cheap

PRINCES' ISLANDS

Ferries to the Princes' Islands leave regularly from Adalar İskelesi, Sirkeci, just beyond the Eminönü jetties, and from Kabataş İskelesi in summer. They call at Kınalı, Burgaz, Heybeliada and Büyükada.

✚ K13 ✉ Adalar İskelesi, Sirkeci ☎ 244 4233 ⏲ Times displayed at jetty 🍴 Snack bar 🚌 Eminönü ♿ None 🖐 Cheap

ÜSKÜDAR

Ferries cross the Bosphorus from Eminönü to Üsküdar at approximately 15-minute intervals. From here you can pick up the local ferry to Beşiktaş.

✚ K12 ✉ Eminönü İskelesi 2, Eminönü ☎ 528 4456 ⏲ Times displayed at jetty 🍴 Snack bar 🚌 Eminönü ♿ None 🖐 Cheap

MAUSOLEUMS

See Top 25 Sights for
BAYEZID II ➤ 29
EYÜP ENSARI ➤ 25
SÜLEYMAN THE MAGNIFICENT ➤ 28

GÜLNUŞ EMETULLAH SULTAN

Built by Sultan Ahmed III as the last resting place of his mother, this beautiful mausoleum dates from 1710 and has an unusual birdcage roof, delicate pointed arches (known as ogives) and wrought-iron grilles.
➕ J16 ✉ Yeni Valide Camii, Hakimiyet-i Milliye Caddesi, Üsküdar 🍴 Nearby cafés (£) and restaurants (££) ⛴ Üsküdar İskelesi ♿ None 🎫 Free

KOCA SINAN PAŞA

The tomb of the grand vizier of Murat III was designed by the sultan's chief architect, Davut Ağa, in 1593. The 16-sided mausoleum is of white- and rose-coloured stone, with a striking stalactite cornice.
➕ L12 ✉ Yeniçeriler Caddesi, Divanyolu 🕐 Hours of prayer 🍴 Cafés near by (£) 🚋 Beyazıt ♿ None 🎫 Free, gratuity

MAHMUT II

This impressive, octagonal mausoleum was designed in the French Empire style by Garabet Balyan in 1839. Take a stroll through the cemetery to see some fine examples of Ottoman tombstones.
➕ L12 ✉ Divanyolu Caddesi, Sultanahmet 🕐 Wed–Sun 9:30–4:30 🍴 Cafés on Divan Yolu Caddesi (£) 🚋 Çemberlitaş ♿ None 🎫 Free, gratuity

MAHMUT PAŞA

This exquisite tomb was built in the late 15th century to honour Mehmet the Conqueror's grand vizier, who, despite his Turkish name, actually hailed from Serbia. Particularly eye-catching are the geometric blue, gold and turquoise mosaic patterns on the façade.
➕ L12 ✉ Vezirhanı Caddesi, Mahmutpaşa 🕐 On request 🍴 Nearby cafés (£) ♿ None 🎫 Free

SINAN THE ARCHITECT

There can be no more fitting memorial to the architect of the Süleymaniye Camii than this modest mausoleum, which stands in what used to be the garden of his house.
➕ K11 ✉ Mimar Sinan Caddesi, Süleymaniye 🕐 Hours of prayer ♿ None 🎫 Free, gratuity

Ceramic gardens

One of the glories of Islamic art, tile-making flourished in İznik (north-western Turkey) from the late 15th to the early 17th centuries. The workshops produced tiles to order following designs prepared by the sultans' artists. In mausoleums and mosques, floral motifs (tulips, peonies, hyacinths and roses) are particularly common. To the faithful, these 'ceramic gardens' suggested the paradise promised in the Koran.

Mausoleum of Grand Vizier Mahmut Paşa

VIEWS

See Top 25 Sights for
TOPKAPI SARAYI ► 42
YEDIKULE CASTLE ► 24

Pierre Loti Café

The French writer and sometime naval officer, Pierre Loti, was captivated by Constantinople when he lived here in the 19th century; this was one of his favourite haunts, with views over the Golden Horn (✚ E8 ✉ Karyağdı Sokak, Eyüp ☎ 581 2696 ☺ Daily 10AM–11PM).

ANADOLU KAVAĞI

This impressive ruined fortress, of Byzantine origin, offers outstanding views of the Black Sea and the European shore of the Bosphorus.

✚ Off map at C20 ✉ Anadolu Kavağı ☺ Daily 🛥 Anadolu Kavağı İskelesi 🚫 None 💷 Free

BÜYÜK ÇAMLICA

Climb 'Great Pine Mountain' (268m above sea-level) to look over the Golden Horn and Sea of Marmara.

✚ J21 ✉ Büyükçamlıca Tepesi 🍴 Café and teahouse 🛥 Üsküdar, then taxi 🚫 None 💷 Free

GALATA TOWER

One of the most conspicuous landmarks of Istanbul, the 140m-high Galata Tower was built in 1348 and used as a watchtower. Spectacular sunsets.

✚ J12 ✉ Büyükhendek Sokak, Tünel ☎ 245 1160 ☺ Daily 8AM–9PM 🍴 Restaurant (£££) 🚇 Tünel 🚫 Good 💷 Moderate

The view from the Galata Tower

ST GEORGE'S MONASTERY

From the grounds of the tiny 10th-century monastery, atop Yüce Tepe Hill, there are views over the islands and eastern Istanbul.

✚ Off map ✉ Büyükada (Princes' Islands) ☺ Daily 🍴 Restaurant open for lunch 🚫 None 💷 Free

SERAGLIO POINT

With superb views across the Bosphorus, Seraglio Point lies at the northern end of Gülhane Park, formerly the rose garden of Topkapı Palace.

✚ K13 ✉ Gülhane Parkı, Kennedy Caddesi, Sarayburnu ☺ Daily 🍴 Café 🚇 Gülhane 🚫 None 💷 Free

YAVUZ SELIM CAMII

From the terrace of the mausoleum of Selim, Süleyman the Magnificent's father, you can look across the Golden Horn and old town.

✚ J10 ✉ Yavuz Selim Caddesi, Fatih ☺ Daily, hours of prayer 🚫 None 💷 Free

FOUNTAINS

See Top 25 Sights for
WILHELM II FOUNTAIN, AT MEYDANI
(HIPPODROME) ➤ 36

AYASOFYA ABLUTION FOUNTAIN
This exquisite fountain, dating from 1740, decorates the courtyard of Ayasofya. Look out for the carved capitals on the columns and the intricate calligraphic patterns etched in bronze beneath the eaves of the single-domed roof.
➕ L13 ☒ Ayasofya Meydanı, Sultanahmet ⏰ Tue–Sun 9:30–5 🚃 Sultanahmet 🚫 None 🅿 Moderate

ESMA SULTAN NAMAZGÂHI AND FOUNTAIN
The marble staircase at the side of this handsome ablution fountain was built for the devout who came here to pray. Ironically, the donor, Esma Sultan, was renowned for her lasciviousness – after tiring of her slave lovers she is said to have had them drowned.
➕ M12 ☒ Kadırga Limanı Caddesi 🚉 Kumkapı
🚫 None 🅿 Free

FOUNTAIN OF AHMET III
This rococo fountain, near the entrance to Topkapı Palace, is perhaps the finest in Istanbul. One of many extravagances built at the behest of the Tulip Sultan, Ahmed III, its decoration is exuberant, with bands of coloured marbles, floral reliefs and calligraphic patterning. The inscription reads 'Turn on the tap, drink the water and pray for the house of Ahmed.'
➕ L13 ☒ Babıhumayun Caddesi, Sultanahmet
⏰ Daily 🚫 None 🅿 Free

FOUNTAIN OF AHMED III IN ÜSKÜDAR
Visitors leaving the ferry at Üsküdar can hardly fail to see this model of architectural restraint, built by Sultan Ahmed III in memory of his mother, Gülnuş Emetullah Sultan, who is buried near by. The sultan himself was responsible for some of the inscriptions.
➕ J16 ☒ Hakimiyet-i Milliye Meydanı 🚢 Üsküdar İskelesi 🚫 None 🅿 Free

KÜÇÜKSU FOUNTAIN ➤ 54

TOPKAPI FOUNTAIN
This lovely drinking fountain adorns the portico of Sultan Ahmed III's library and was built by the architect Sinan in 1578. The gilt arabesques inscribed on contrasting blue-grey and orange marble are its most striking feature.
➕ L13 ☒ Third Courtyard, Topkapı Sarayı
⏰ Wed–Mon 9–5 ☎ Café (££), restaurant (£££; ➤ 62)
🚃 Gülhane 🚫 None 🅿 Moderate

Şadırvan
At the last count there were 491 public fountains in Istanbul, more than a quarter of them endowed by the women of the harem. According to the teachings of Islam, donating an ablution fountain (şadırvan) was a religious act pleasing in the sight of Allah. A typical inscription reads 'the mother of Ali Paşa Vezir in the reign of Sultan Mahmut quenched the thirst of the people with the pure and clear water of her charity'.

Detail from the fountain of Ahmet III

FOR CHILDREN

Getting away

With its crowds and narrow streets, Istanbul can be very trying for children, especially after a heavy morning's sightseeing. Why not get away from it all by taking them to one of the many beaches in the area? Try Kilyos on the Black Sea (► 21) or one of the resorts on the Sea of Marmara.

Military Museum bandsman

BAYRAMOĞLU BIRD PARK AND BOTANIC GARDENS ► 21
Ideal for nature lovers, this park has exotic birds and animals as well as hundreds of tropical plants.

BÜYÜKADA ISLAND ► 20
Motorised transport is forbidden here – take a horse and trap rather than a taxi!

CARICATURE AND HUMOUR MUSEUM
Located in the shadow of the Aqueduct of Valens, this fascinating museum holds caricature workshops.
🕂 K11 🖂 Atatürk Bulvarı, Kovacılar Sokak 12, Fatih ☎ 521 1264 🕔 Daily 9:30–5 🍴 Cafés (£) near by 🕭 None 🎟 Cheap

EMINÖNÜ AND BEYAZIT SQUARES
Buy corn to feed the pigeons in Beyazıt Square (► 29), or browse in the flower and pet market behind the Yeni Camii at Eminönü (► 51).

FERRIES ► 44 AND 56
Even if you only have an hour to spare, you can take a trip to Üsküdar and back. Children will love it.

FISH MARKET AT EMINÖNÜ
Watch the fishermen selling their catches, or sample some yourself. Along the waterfront, you will also see hawkers demonstrating household gadgets and toys.
🕂 K12 🖂 Eminönü İskelesi, Eminönü 🕔 Daily 🍴 Snack bars (£) 🚈 Eminönü 🕭 None 🎟 Free

MILITARY MUSEUM ► 55
Visit on a summer afternoon and be entertained by a historic Janissary band.

MISIR ÇARŞISI (SPICE BAZAAR) ► 32
Wander from shop to shop trying the samples of delicious Turkish delight – absolutely free of charge!

TATILYA EĞLENCE MERKEZI (THE REPUBLIC OF FUN)
'Istanbul's Disneyland', with roller-coasters, a simulation cinema and 12 theme units.
🕂 Off map at K7 🖂 Beylikdüzü Mevkii, Büyükçekmece ☎ 872 5530 🕔 Daily 🍴 Cafés (£) and restaurants (££) 🕭 None 🎟 Moderate

YEDIKULE CASTLE ► 24, ANADOLU KAVAĞI ► 58, RUMELI HISARI ► 54
You can explore the grounds and even climb onto the walls and battlements of these medieval castle ruins. But be careful as there are few railings or safety barriers.

ISTANBUL
where to...

TURKISH HAUTE CUISINE

Tasty Turkish dishes

Arnavut ciğeri – spicy liver with onions.

Çerkez tavuğu – chicken in walnut purée.

Döner kebab – lamb grilled on a spit.

İç pilav – rice with nuts, currants and onions.

İmam bayaldı – aubergines with tomatoes and onions.

Mantı – ravioli with yoghurt.

Piyaz – haricot bean salad.

Sigara böreği – fried filo pastry filled with cheese.

Şiş köfte – grilled meatballs.

Su böreği – baked pastry filled with meat or cheese.

Tas kebab – not a kebab, but a meat and vegetable stew.

Yaprak dolma – stuffed vine leaves.

ASITANE (£££)

Convenient for visiting the Kariye Mosque, this expensive but reputable hotel restaurant presents *nouvelle* Ottoman cuisine to the accompaniment of classical Turkish music (evenings only). Outdoor service in the garden during summer.
H9 ⊠ Kariye Hotel, Kariye Camii Sokak 18, Edirnekapı ☎ 534 8414 Daily 12–3, 7:30–11

DEVELI (££)

Established in 1912, this excellent Turkish restaurant sells wonderful meat dishes, including *patlıcanlı kebab* (kebab with aubergine) and *fıstıklı kebab* (kebab with pistachios). Terrace open in the summer.
M9 ⊠ Balık Pazarı, Gümüşyüzük Sokak 7, Samatya ☎ 529 0833/34 Daily noon–midnight

ECE (££)

Named after local Turkish gourmet, Ece Hanım, who prepares superb Turkish dishes with an unusual emphasis on herbs and vegetables. The views of the Bosphorus are a bonus.
Off map at C19 ⊠ Tramvay Caddesi 104, Kuruçeşme ☎ 265 9600 Mon–Sat 6PM–2AM

KONYALI (££)

Traditional Turkish cuisine, including *börek* and kebab, is served in this restaurant in the grounds of Topkapı Palace. It's worth trying to get here early as space is at a premium after 1PM, when tour parties descend. The atmosphere is elegant and fairly formal.
L13 ⊠ Topkapı Sarayı, Sultanahmet ☎ 513 9696 Wed–Mon 10–4.30 Sultanahmet

REŞAT PAŞA KONAĞI (££)

Excellent Turkish and Ottoman dishes are served in this turn-of-the-century Turkish villa. Summer garden and live music, Thursday to Saturday.
Off map at O20 ⊠ Sinan Ercan Caddesi 34/1, Erenköy ☎ (216) 361 3411 Daily 7:30PM–11PM

SARNIÇ RESTAURANT (££)

Authentic Ottoman cuisine and wonderful international dishes in a converted Roman cistern, which lends itself to an attractive ambience.
L13 ⊠ Soğukçeşme Caddesi, Sultanahmet ☎ 512 4291 Tue–Sun 12–3, 8–midnight Gülhane

TOPKAPI RESTAURANT (£££)

Succulent Turkish dishes are the mainstay of this restaurant. There is a barbecue every day except Sunday, and Turkish gypsy music and dancing three days a week.
L13 ⊠ Eresin Topkapı İstanbul Hotel, Topkapı ☎ 631 1212 Daily 7PM–midnight Topkapı

RESTAURANTS WITH A VIEW

ALI BABA (££)

This no-frills fish restaurant with a Bosphorus location has been operating since the 1920s, serving a range of grills, stews and *mezes*. There is outdoor seating in the summer.

➕ Off map at C19 ✉ Kireçburnu Caddesi 20, Kireçburnu ☎ 262 0889 🕐 Daily noon–midnight

THE DINING ROOM (££)

Turkish and international dishes served high above the Bosphorus.

➕ G13 ✉ Hotel Gezi, Mete Caddesi Taksim ☎ 251 7430 🕐 Daily 11–11

FERIYE RESTAURANT (£££)

A pricey but reliable international restaurant with live jazz on Wednesdays, Fridays and Saturdays and an attractive terrace with views across the Bosphorus.

➕ F17 ✉ Çırağan Caddesi 124, Beşiktaş ☎ 259 2487 🕐 Daily 11AM–midnight 🚇 Beşiktaş

HUZUR (££)

Wonderful views of the Bosphorus from this excellent fish restaurant. Try shrimps cooked in an earthenware casserole.

➕ D18 ✉ Sahilhane Sokak 21, Arnavutköy ☎ 263 4219 🕐 Daily 11–11

INCI RESTAURANT AND CAFÉ (£££)

A fish restaurant with superb views of Topkapı and the Bosphorus. Plain drinks and snacks are served in the café.

➕ K15 ✉ Salacak Sahil Yolu 1, Üsküdar ☎ (216) 341 9450 🕐 Daily 10AM–11PM 🚇 Üsküdar

KURUÇEŞME DIVAN LOKANTASI (£££)

Turkish and French cuisine served on a beautiful terrace with magnificent views of the Bosphorus.

➕ D18 ✉ Kuruçeşme Caddesi, Kuruçeşme ☎ 257 7150 🕐 Daily 12–3, 7–11 (Sun brunch 8AM–1PM)

RAMI (££)

Dedicated to the memory of the Impressionist artist Ressam Rami Uluer, this traditional Turkish restaurant opened in 1989 and is becoming increasingly popular with tourists, not only for its food but for its 19th-century Ottoman décor and the wonderful views of the Blue Mosque.

➕ M13 ✉ Utangaç Sokak 6, Sultanahmet ☎ 517 6593 🕐 Daily 11–midnight

SUMMIT RESTAURANT (£££)

This rooftop restaurant has superb views of the Bosphorus and Yıldız imperial gardens.

➕ F16 ✉ Conrad International Hotel, Yıldız Caddesi Beşiktaş ☎ 227 3000 🕐 Daily 12–midnight

Ortaköy dining

Ortaköy, one of Istanbul's liveliest and most colourful districts, has a waterfront lined with cafés and terrace restaurants that boast superb views of the Bosphorus and of the exquisite 19th-century Ortaköy Mosque. You can choose from Turkish, Italian, Mexican and international menus, although the local fish is the speciality. A street market draws the crowds on Sundays and there are craft and junk shops to explore.

SEAFOOD RESTAURANTS

Fish street

The ancient harbour of Kumkapı has the highest concentration of fish restaurants in Istanbul (there are well over 50 in all). There are spectacular views of the Marmara from Kennedy Caddesi, but if it's atmosphere you are looking for, head for the narrow streets behind the railway station where the tables spill out onto the pavements and where the restaurateurs vie with one another in the noisy promotion of their wares.

ASIR (£)

Much frequented by Istanbul's intellectuals, this fish restaurant gets very crowded in the summer when the outdoor section opens. At other times it may be a trial for non-smokers.
⊞ G13 ⊠ Kalyoncukulluk Caddesi 94/1, Beyoğlu
☎ 250 0557 ⏰ Daily 11–3, 7–midnight
🚇 Tarlabaşı Caddesi

BIRTAT RESTAURANT (££)

Tasty fish dishes are served at this popular waterfront restaurant, located near the jetty on the island of Büyükada. Ideal for lunch.
⊞ Off map ⊠ Gülistan Caddesi 10, Büyükada, Princes' Islands
☎ (216) 382 1245 ⏰ Daily 11–3, 7–11
🚢 Büyükada

BIZIM (££)

Fish *börek* is the speciality at this large tree-shrouded restaurant on the Bosphorus. *Kalamar* and shrimp in butter are also on the menu.
⊞ Off map at C19 ⊠ Kefeliköy Caddesi 27, Kireçburnu ☎ 262 0504 ⏰ Daily 7–midnight

BOĞAZIÇI BALIK (£££)

On the expensive side, but it is worth treating yourself to some of the excellent fish dishes, which include fish balls and 'oysters in the oven'.
⊞ Off map at C19 ⊠ Köybaşı Caddesi 10, Yeniköy ☎ 262 0071 ⏰ Daily noon–midnight 🚢 Yeniköy

DENIZ KIZI (££)

The hearty fish platter is very modestly priced; try starting with the fried fresh anchovies and mullet.
⊞ Off map at C19 ⊠ Balıkçılar Çarşısı, Sarıyer ☎ 242 8570 ⏰ Daily 11–3, 7–midnight 🚢 Sarıyer

DENIZ KIZI MARINA RESTAURANT (££)

A popular fish restaurant with live music nightly. Meat dishes are also available.
⊞ Off map at C19 ⊠ Yeniköy Caddesi 38, Tarabya ☎ 262 8808 ⏰ Daily 11–3, 7–1

HASAN BALIKÇILAR LOKANTASI (£££)

Reputed to be one of the best fish restaurants in Istanbul. Try finishing your meal with the baked quince and clotted cream.
⊞ Off map at O7 ⊠ Yat Limanı, Rıhtım Sokak 8, Yeşilköy ☎ 573 8300 ⏰ Daily noon–midnight

ISMAIL'IN YERII (£)

The fried mussels are exceptional in this three-storey fish restaurant in beautiful Anadolu Kavağı.
⊞ Off map at C19 ⊠ Eğriboyun Sokak 7, Anadolu Kavağı ☎ (216) 320 2136 ⏰ Daily 11–11 🚢 Anadolu Kavağı

KEMAL BALIK RESTAURANT (££)

This friendly fish restaurant was opened by the present owner's grandfather back in 1903 and is one of the more reliable Kumkapı establishments.

✚ M11 ✉ Üstad Sokak, Kumkapı ☎ 517 6069 ⏲ Daily 11AM–midnight 🚇 Kumkapı

KIYI (££)

The shrimp with mushroom is especially recommended at this popular seaside restaurant.
✚ Off map at C19 ✉ Kefeliköy Caddesi 126, Tarabya ☎ 262 0002 ⏲ Daily noon–midnight

KÖR AGOP (£££)

This stylish *meyhane* is one of the most sought-after eateries in Kumkapı's ' fish district'. Specialities include gurnard soup and oven-cooked shrimp casserole.
✚ M11 ✉ Kumkapı Meydanı ☎ 517 2334 ⏲ Daily 11–3, 6–midnight 🚇 Kumkapı

KÖRFEZ (£££)

A smart waterfront restaurant with a summer garden, serving excellent fish dishes including the house speciality – sea bass cooked in salt.
✚ Off map at C20 ✉ Körfez Caddesi 78, Kanlıca ☎ (216) 413 4314 ⏲ Tue–Sun 12–3, 7–midnight 🚢 Kanlıca

KUYU RESTAURANT (££)

A long-established restaurant, renowned locally for its poached fish.
✚ C19 ✉ 1 Caddesi 31/3, Arnavutköy ☎ 263 6750 ⏲ Daily 7–midnight

LE PECHEUR (£££)

A large, attractive fish restaurant with wonderful sea views and a delightful summer garden for alfresco dining.
✚ Off map at C19 ✉ Yeniköy Caddesi 80, Tarabya ☎ 262 7070 ⏲ Daily noon–midnight

MARINA BALIK RESTAURANT (£££)

Occupying an old ferry landing stage, Marina Balık offers a wide variety of seafood dishes as well as live guitar music some evenings.
✚ D18 ✉ Vapur İskelesi, Kuruçeşme ☎ 287 2653 ⏲ Daily 7–midnight

PAYSAGE (£££)

There is a 20 per cent discount on the evening menu in this hillside restaurant serving excellent fish dishes. Bosphorus views.
✚ Off map at C20 ✉ Hekimler Sitesi, Kanlıca ☎ (216) 322 7060 ⏲ Daily 11–3, 7–midnight 🚢 Kanlıca

RUMELI ISKELE RESTAURANT (££)

Tasty fish dishes in this restaurant near the famous castle.
✚ Off map at C19 ✉ Yahya Kemal Caddesi 1, Rumeli Hisarı ☎ 263 2997 ⏲ Daily 11–3, 7–11

YEDI GÜN (££)

Delicious shrimp casserole and other delicacies are on offer at this friendly restaurant located at the far end of the Bosphorus. Very popular at the weekends.
✚ Off map at C19 ✉ Rumeli Kavağı ☎ 242 3798 ⏲ Daily noon–11PM 🚢 Rumeli Kavağı

Fisherman's catch

Balık – fish
Hamsi – anchovy
İstavrit – mackerel
Kalamar – squid
Karides – prawns
Kılıç – swordfish
Levrek – bass
Lüfer – blue fish
Midye – mussels
Palamut/torik – bonito
Tekir – mullet
Yengeç – crab

EVERYDAY TURKISH

Mezes

In the typical Istanbul restaurant, you will be offered a selection of hot and cold appetisers known collectively as *mezes*. They can range from simple salads dressed in olive oil to aubergine purée and Çengelköy cucumbers, and from *biber dolması* (green peppers stuffed with raisins, rice and pinenuts) to fried *kalamar* with *tarator* (breadcrumbs flavoured with garlic and walnut), Albanian diced liver and pastries seasoned with fresh herbs. *Mezes* are usually accompanied by servings of fresh white bread.

À LA TURKA (£)
This small Turkish restaurant, in charming Ortaköy, specialises in dishes like *gözleme* (stuffed pastry) and *mantı* (ravioli). There is a large salad bar but no alcoholic drinks are served. Outdoor seating during the summer.
➕ F18 ✉ Hazine Sokak 8, Ortaköy ☎ 258 7924 🕙 Daily 10AM–10.30PM 🚢 Ortaköy Vapur İskelesi

DARÜZZIYAF (££)
Traditional Turkish cuisine served in the delightful surroundings of the Süleymaniye *imaret*. Lovely garden, too.
➕ K11 ✉ Darüzziyafiye Şifahane Caddesi 6, Süleymaniye ☎ 511 8414 🕙 Daily 10AM–11PM

DEEP RESTAURANT (£)
An unassuming but friendly Turkish restaurant with a resourceful chef. The prices are reasonable, which attracts the mainly youthful clientele.
➕ H13 ✉ Kurabiye Sokak 2, Beyoğlu ☎ 244 0839 🕙 Daily 7–12 🚇 İstiklâl Caddesi

GM RESTAURANT (££)
The specialities of the house are meat dishes and home-style cooking from south-eastern Anatolia.
➕ Off map at C16 ✉ Hacı Adil Caddesi 4. Aralık Sokak 1/2, Levent ☎ 281 2762 🕙 Daily 12–3, 6:30–midnight

KONAK RESTAURANT (£)
This no-nonsense Turkish eatery, located near the Hippodrome, has a restaurant on the first floor. Visitors choose from a wide variety of dishes, including kebabs, meatballs, omelettes and chicken rolls, from the counter downstairs.
➕ L12 ✉ Divan Yolu Caddesi 66–8, Sultanahmet ☎ 526 8933 🕙 Daily 8AM–midnight 🚇 Sultanahmet

OTEL ALZER RESTAURANT (£)
The Alzer is ideally situated for visitors to the Hippodrome and the Blue Mosque. The cuisine is traditional Ottoman.
➕ M12 ✉ At Meydanı 72 Sultanahmet ☎ 516 6262 🕙 10AM–midnight 🚇 Sultanahmet

PANDELI (££)
Located in the former guardhouse of the Spice Bazaar and beautifully decorated with blue ceramic tiles, Pandeli Usta's famous restaurant offers more than 70 dishes, including sea bass *en papillotte* and aubergine *börek*.
➕ K12 ✉ Mısır Çarşısı 1, Eminönü ☎ 527 3909 🕙 Mon–Sat 10–4:30PM 🚢 Eminönü

PAVYON (££)
A friendly restaurant in the famous 'Flowers Passage', serving a wide variety of typical Turkish *mezes*. Very lively in the evenings, with ethnic folk-music accompaniment.
➕ H13 ✉ Tarihi Çiçek Pasajı, Galatasaray ☎ 249 3957 🕙 Daily 11–3, 6–midnight 🚇 İstiklâl Caddesi

INTERNATIONAL RESTAURANTS

FOUR SEASONS (££)

For more than 20 years this first-rate English-run restaurant has been serving inventive and attractively presented international dishes to satisfied customers. A restrained ambience in an excellent central location.

✚ J12 ⊠ İstiklâl Caddesi 509, Tünel ☎ 293 3941 ⏲ Daily 12–3, 6–midnight 🚇 Tünel 🚌 İstiklâl Caddesi

GUANG ZHOU (£££)

This Chinese restaurant is known for its devoted Chinese clientéle. Expensive if you eat *à la carte*, but you can economise with the lunch specials or the set meals in the evening.

✚ G13 ⊠ İnönü Caddesi 53, Taksim ☎ 243 6379 ⏲ Daily 12–3, 6–11:30 🚌 İstiklâl Caddesi

LE SELECT (£££)

Reservations are essential if you want a table at this exclusive gourmet restaurant. The main dishes are international but it's the starters that people rave about.

✚ Off map at C16 ⊠ Manolya Sokak 21, Levent ☎ 268 2120 ⏲ Daily 12–3PM, 8PM–1AM

LEBANESE RESTAURANT (£££)

The only authentic Lebanese restaurant in Istanbul; fresh, tasty dishes including *tajen* (stews), *felafel* and *mekanek*.

✚ G13 ⊠ Lamartin Caddesi 41, Taksim ☎ 250 2071 ⏲ Daily 12–3, 7–midnight

LES AMBASSADEURS (£££)

A formal restaurant with views of the Bosphorus, famous for its Russian *haute cuisine*, including a wide range of *zakuski* and frozen vodka. Also Turkish dishes.

✚ Off map at C19 ⊠ Bebek Hotel, Cevdet Paşa Caddesi 113– 5, Bebek ☎ 263 3002 ⏲ Daily 12–3:30, 7–midnight

MARMIT (££)

Book in advance if you want to be sure of a table at this popular bistro specialising in Mexican and South American cuisine.

✚ Off map at O7 ⊠ Yeşilköy Marina ☎ 573 8581 ⏲ Daily 7:30PM–midnight

METSOU-YAN (££)

Unique to Istanbul, this restaurant – in an historic part of the city – serves authentic Jewish kosher food.

✚ L11 ⊠ Hotel Merit Antique, Ordu Caddesi 238, Laleli ☎ 513 9300 ⏲ Sat–Thu 7PM–11PM 🚌 Laleli

SAI THAI (£££)

The ingredients are fresh, the cuisine and setting authentic, and the service immaculate, in this first-rate Thai restaurant.

✚ Off map at C16 ⊠ Aytar Caddesi, Levent İşhanı 3/6, Birinci Levent ☎ 283 5346 ⏲ Tue–Sun 12–3, 6:30–11

Bortsch on the Bosphorus

Russian emigrés fleeing the Revolution flooded Istanbul in the early 1920s, bringing with them a demand for home-grown cooking. Most of the eating houses that sprung up all over Pera have long since disappeared, but the influence of Russian cuisine can still be seen in the menus of international restaurants such as Les Ambassadeurs. You'll find *bortsch, blini* and *caviare* among the hors-d'oeuvres, and such standard main courses as chicken Kiev and beef Stroganoff. Vodka is also widely available.

SNACKS

Take-aways

Snacks are a speciality of Istanbul's street traders. If you are on the waterfront, you'll find the barbecued mackerel (served in rolls) irresistible. Equally popular with the Turks are bread rings covered in sesame seeds, known locally as *simit*. You'll also find salad rolls, kebabs and *lahmacun* – a kind of pizza with a meat topping – on offer. *Börek* (a pastry with meat or cheese) is sold from hand carts as well as in cafés. In summer you may be happy to make do with an ice-cream (*dondurma*).

ARCHAEOLOGICAL MUSEUM CAFÉ (£)
The café is in the garden courtyard, where you will be surrounded by ancient statues and busts from the museum collection.
⊞ L13 ⊠ Gülhane Park, Eminönü ☎ 520 7740 ⓘ Summer only Tue–Sun 11–3 🚇 Gülhane

ASIRLIK KANLICA YOĞURDU (£)
Kanlıca is famous for its yoghurt, which is the chief attraction of this waterfront café with excellent views of the Bosphorus.
⊞ Off map at C20 ⊠ İskele Yanı 2, Kanlıca ☎ (216) 413 4469 ⓘ Daily 9–9 🚢 Kanlıca

BASILICA CISTERN CAFÉ (£)
Relax in the cavernous surroundings of the famous Byzantine cistern. An experience not to be missed!
⊞ L13 ⊠ Yerebatan Sarayı, Yerebatan Caddesi 13, Sultanahmet ☎ 522 1259 ⓘ Daily 10–5 🚇 Sultanahmet

ÇUKUR CAFÉ (£)
If you are overcome with exhaustion from shopping in the antique shops of Çukurcuma, this is an ideal place to sit down for a cup of tea and a rest.
⊞ H13 ⊠ Faik Paşa Caddesi 37, Çukurcuma ☎ 244 5114 ⓘ Daily 8:30AM–6PM

HOUSE OF MEDUSA CAFÉ RESTAURANT (£)
An ideal stopover for visitors to the Blue Mosque or the Basilica Cistern, this friendly café serves grills, chicken dishes and kebabs, all with chips if you must.
⊞ L13 ⊠ Muhterem Efendi Sokak 19, Yerebatan Caddesi, Sultanahmet ☎ 511 4116 ⓘ Daily 9AM–6PM 🚇 Sultanahmet

KANAAT (£)
A modest but dependable no-frills *lokanta*, founded in 1933. Kanaat sells standard Turkish fare at very reasonable prices.
⊞ J17 ⊠ Selmanı Pak Caddesi 25, Üsküdar ☎ 333 3791 ⓘ Daily 10:30AM–10:30PM 🚢 Üsküdar

LITTLE CHINA (£)
A typical Chinese take-away restaurant with a few tables indoors.
⊞ Off map at C16 ⊠ Tepecik Yolu, Alkent Alışveriş Merkezi, Etiler ☎ 263 1715 ⓘ Wed–Mon noon–11PM

NEXT CAFÉ (£)
Serves a delicious variety of cheesecakes, tarts, pies and ice-creams, but also salads, *böreks* and chicken dishes.
⊞ F14 ⊠ Ihlamur Yolu 3/1, Nişantaşı ☎ 247 8043 ⓘ Daily 8AM–11PM

OPERA CAFÉ (£)
A conveniently located sandwich bar, serving cold sandwiches as well as *döner*, hamburgers and salads.
⊞ H14 ⊠ İnönü Caddesi 73/A, Taksim ☎ 245 2042 ⓘ Daily 9AM–9PM

BEST OF THE REST

AKGÜN MAYNA (££)
Views of the marina (if
you arrive early) as you
tuck into the deep- fried
meatballs with cracked
wheat crust, beef stew
with aubergine purée,
baklava and *kadayif*.
➕ Off map at O7
✉ Ataköy Marina, Ataköy
☎ 560 8010 🕐 Daily
11–11

CAFÉ AMADEUS (££)
The Austrian patron of this
well-known restaurant
prides herself on her
schnitzel, *apfelstrudel* and
sachertorte. The setting is
an attractive villa with a
summer garden.
➕ Off map at C16
✉ Karanfil Sokak 39,
Levent ☎ 269 5686
🕐 Tue–Sun 11–11

GELIK (££)
A large, informal café-
restaurant with sea views,
very popular with the
locals. There is a wide
selection of Turkish
dishes, including spit-
roasted lamb, *döner* and
ayran.
➕ Off map at O7
✉ Sahilyolu, Mobil
Karşısı, Ataköy
☎ 560 7282 🕐 Daily
10AM–midnight

NATURE & PEACE (££)
This centrally located
restaurant offers
health-food dishes made
to order. The service is
slow but the food is worth
waiting for.
➕ H13 ✉ İstiklâl
Caddesi,
Büyükparmakkapı Sokak
21, Beyoğlu ☎ 252 8609
🕐 Daily 10AM–11PM
🚇 İstiklâl Caddesi

KARABIBER (£)
Owned by a foundation
aiming to promote
traditional women's work,
this restaurant offers a
wide variety of Turkish
regional dishes.
➕ J12 ✉ General
Yazgan Sokak 3, Tünel
☎ 251 9085 🕐 Mon–Sat
9–6:30 🚇 Tünel

TARIHI SULTANAHMET KÖFTECISI (£)
Honest Turkish fare in
unlimited quantities – the
chef encourages second
and even third helpings!
➕ L12 ✉ Divan Yolu 12,
Sultanahmet ☎ 513 1438
🕐 Daily 10AM–11PM
🚇 Sultanahmet

TRIEZE (£££)
The main attractions here
are the unusual game
dishes, including pheasant,
partridge, quail and venison
(subject to availability).
The location, near
Yeşilköy Marina, is a bonus.
➕ Off map at O7
✉ Çamözü Sokak 13,
Yeşilköy ☎ 663 5531
🕐 Daily 11–3, 7–midnight

TÜRKISTAN AŞEVI (££)
Located in a picturesque
wooden mansion dating
back to 1843, this
welcoming restaurant
specialises in the cuisine
of Turkestan, including
buttered pancakes (served
with spinach, cheese or
meat), *mantı* and *samsa*.
The floors are covered
with handmade carpets, so
visitors are requested to
leave their shoes by the
door. No alcohol.
➕ M13 ✉ Tavukhane
Sokağı 36, Sultanahmet
☎ 518 1344 🕐 Daily 7–11

Beer
Beer only became a
popular drink in Turkey at
the end of the 19th
century. The first Istanbul
brewery opened in Şişli in
1893 and was owned by
the Swiss Bomonti
brothers. The outside
beer garden became an
immediate hit with the
locals, but it was not until
1933 that the founder of
the republic, Kemal
Atatürk, opened the first
national brewery. The
leading firm today is Efes
Pilsen, a private concern
which was founded in
1969. It currently
accounts for 73 per cent
of Turkish beer
production and exports to
more than 30 countries.

CARPETS & KILIMS

The hard sell

There are no more accomplished practitioners of the 'hard sell' than the carpet merchants of Istanbul. A favourite technique is to waylay unsuspecting carousers returning late at night from restaurants or nightclubs and invite them into the shop for a nightcap (usually no stronger than apple tea). Two or three hours later, the weary 'guest' emerges as a customer laden with carpets.

A LA TURCA
Pricey but reliable purveyor of carpets and kilims.
🕂 F15 ☒ Conrad International Hotel, Beşiktaş ☎ 227 3583 ⊕ Mon–Sat 9:30–6

ADNAN HASSAN
A good selection of carpets and kilims in this shop in the heart of the carpet district of the Covered Bazaar.
🕂 L12 ☒ Kapalı Çarşı, Halıcılar Sokağı 90, Beyazıt ⊕ Mon–Sat 8:30–7 🚇 Çemberlitaş

ANTIKART
Strictly for connoisseurs, this store specialises in antique and rare kilims.
🕂 H13 ☒ İstiklâl Caddesi 209, Atlas Kuyumcular Çarşısı Beyoğlu ☎ 252 4482 ⊕ Mon–Sat 9:30–6 🚇 İstiklâl Caddesi

ANTIKHANE
This large warehouse in the centre of the 'antique-selling district' has a good selection of carpets, kilims and textiles.
🕂 H13 ☒ Resto Han Faikpaşa Yokuşu 41, Çukurcuma ☎ 251 9587 ⊕ Mon–Sat 9:30–6

ARASTA BAZAAR
Situated just outside the walls of the Blue Mosque, this row of shops offers a selection of old and new carpets and kilims.
🕂 M13 ☒ Kabasakal Caddesi, Sultanahmet ⊕ Daily 10–8

BAZAAR 54
A wide-ranging selection of old and new carpets in a modern shopping mall on the coast road just outside the old city.
🕂 Off map at O7 ☒ Galleria Shopping Mall, Ataköy ☎ 559 0319 ⊕ Mon–Sat 9:30–6

DURUSEL
This internationally renowned company, with branches in New York and Zurich, has an impressive selection of carpets and kilims, and also sells bags and shoes made from the same material. Showroom at the Hilton Hotel.
🕂 L12 ☒ Piyerloti Caddesi, Durusel İşhanı 2, Çemberlitaş ☎ 518 2535 ⊕ Mon–Sat 9:30–6 🚇 Çemberlitaş

HAZAL HALI
An attractive display of carpets and kilims on the waterfront in Ortaköy.
🕂 F17 ☒ Mecidiyeköy Köprüsü Sokak 27–9, Ortaköy ☎ 261 7233 ⊕ Mon–Sat 9:30–6 🚢 Ortaköy Vapur İskelesi

HERITAGE
Situated in the heart of the old town, this establishment specialises in reproducing antique carpet and kilim designs using natural dyes.
🕂 L13 ☒ Caferiye Sokak 6/A, Sultanahmet ☎ 513 6150 ⊕ Mon–Sat 9:30–6 🚇 Gülhane

KERVAN HALI, ORIENTAL CARPETS
Young people in particular seem drawn to this shop, located in an old *medrese*.
🕂 L12 ☒ Çorlulu Ali Paşa Medresesi 36/5,

Çarşıkapı ☎ 519 2341
🕐 Mon–Sat 9:30–6
🚇 Çemberlitaş

MAY

Has an intriguing
selection of attractive,
locally designed handbags,
wallets, briefcases and
backpacks made from
handwoven kilims.
➕ L12 ✉ Kapalı Çarşı,
Kolancılar Kapısı Sokak 7
🕐 Mon–Sat 8:30–7
🚇 Çemberlitaş

MUHLIS GÜNBATTI

Dazzling displays of
traditional carpets and
kilims, plus Turkic textiles
like *suzani* and *ikat*.
➕ L12 ✉ Kapalı Çarşı,
Perdahçılar Caddesi 48
☎ 511 6562 🕐 Mon–Sat
8:30–7 🚇 Çemberlitaş

PASHA

Before leaving the
confines of the beautiful
Kariye Camii, stop to
admire the handmade rugs
and kilims of this
respected establishment.
➕ H9 ✉ Kariye
Mahallesi, Cami Sokak 8,
Edirnekapı ☎ 534 8071
🕐 Mon–Sat 9:30–6

PUNTO

The premises are a 17th-
century caravanserai, which
is one of the attractions;
the other is the selection of
old and new carpets from
all over Turkey.
➕ L12 ✉ Gazi
Sinanpaşa Sokak 17,
Vezirhanı, Cağaloğlu
☎ 511 0853 🕐 Mon–Sat
9:30–6 🚇 Çemberlitaş

ŞENGÖR

A good selection of quality
carpets and kilims in the

heart of the commercial
area of Istanbul.
➕ G13 ✉ Cumhuriyet
Caddesi 47, Taksim
☎ 235 6140 🕐 Mon–Sat
9:30–6 🚇 Taksim

**ŞENGÖR FCI CARPET
HOUSE**

This is one of the oldest
and best-respected carpet
dealers in Istanbul,
situated among the
antique shops of Nişantaşı.
➕ F14 ✉ Abdi İpekçi
Caddesi, Feyzi Feyzioğlu
Sokak 1/2, Nişantaşı
☎ 247 9170 🕐 Mon–Sat
9:30–6

SENTEZ ISTANBUL

You'll find this well-
known and well-
patronised carpet shop off
Divan Yolu Caddesi.
➕ L12 ✉ Bâb-ı-Âli
Caddesi 15–17, Çağaloğlu
☎ 513 1350 🕐 Mon–Sat
9:30–6 🚇 Güllhane

ŞIŞKO OSMAN

An impressive selection of
antique carpets, kilims,
rugs and *cicims* in the
Covered Bazaar.
➕ L12 ✉ Kapalı Çarşı,
Halıcılar Caddesi 49
☎ 526 1708 🕐 Mon–Sat
8:30–7 🚇 Çemberlitaş

ZEMZEM

'Charlie', as he is known
to his friends, offers an
entertaining induction
course in the art of carpet-
making with no obligation
to buy – but beware his
persuasive powers.
➕ L12 ✉ Binbirdirek,
Meydan Sokak 7/3,
Klodfarer Caddesi,
Sultanahmet ☎ 638 8878
🕐 Mon–Sat 9:30–6
🚇 Sultanahmet

How to become a carpet connoisseur

First, remember that
kilims are woven and
have no pile, while
carpets are knotted.
Second, ask the dealer
whether the dyes are
natural or synthetic –
natural last longer. Third,
inspect the tightness of
the weave – the greater
the number of knots, the
more expensive the
carpet. Finally, take
advice but don't be
browbeaten. Choose the
pattern and colour
scheme that appeal to
you most – after all, it is
you who has to live with
the carpet.

71

FASHION & ACCESSORIES

Turkish chic

Turkish *haute couture*, as represented by top designers like Rifat Özbek and Arif İlhan, is very much part of the European mainstream, but the use of home-grown fabrics such as silk, leather and Angora wool gives it a certain extra chic. To see local fashions at their best, head for the boutiques of Nişantaşı and Teşvikiye on the European side, and Bağdat Caddesi in Asia. You may be able to pick up a bargain if you are here for the sales (*indirim*) in January and July.

DESA
One of several branches of this major clothing chain, which specialises in quality Turkish leatherware.
J12 ✉ Swissôtel The Bosphorus, Maçka ☎ 259 0213 🕐 Mon–Sat 9:30–6

DREAMS DESIGNER
This is a major outlet for the top European designer names in women's clothing, including Givenchy, Ronit Zilha, Morgan and Dolce Vita.
F14 ✉ Mim Kemal Öke Caddesi 11/2, Nişantaşı ☎ 231 4865 🕐 Mon–Sat 9:30–6

HOTİÇ
A store with a large selection of stylish shoes for men and women; also handbags. There is a coffee bar here, too.
F14 ✉ Teşvikiye Caddesi 135/1, Nişantaşı ☎ 247 7455 🕐 Mon–Sat 9:30–6

KAPALI ÇARŞI (COVERED BAZAAR)
There are dozens of outlets specialising in leather goods in the Covered Bazaar, and the prices are competitive. It is also worth looking near by on Vezirhanı Caddesi.
L12 ✉ Nuruosmaniye Sokak, Beyazıt 🕐 Mon–Sat 8:30–7 🚇 Çemberlitaş

KARACA
This is one of Turkey's most reputable producers of woollen sweaters for men and women.
E14 ✉ Matbaaci Osmanbey Sokak, Bekiroğlu İş Merkezi 38, Osmanbey ☎ 233 6101 🕐 Mon–Sat 9:30–6

LEVI'S
This store is one of a number of branches selling the famous brand of American jeans – made in Turkey.
E14 ✉ Halaskârgazi Caddesi 206, Osmanbey ☎ 247 4863 🕐 Mon–Sat 9:30–6

MODELLO
A store selling modish leatherware, with a good line in suede jackets.
Off map at C16 ✉ Nispetiye Caddesi 2/1, Etiler ☎ 257 7465 🕐 Mon–Sat 9:30–6

MUDO COLLECTION
One of Turkey's leading fashion chains selling stylish, high-quality men's and women's casual wear.
F14 ✉ Teşvikiye Caddesi 143, Nişantaşı ☎ 225 2941 🕐 Mon–Sat 9:30–6

TIFFANY-TOMATO
A branch of the popular Turkish chain, selling local fashion for young people.
E14 ✉ Rumeli Caddesi 67, Osmanbey ☎ 241 0845 🕐 Mon–Sat 9:30–6

VAKKO
This store sells men's and women's fashions in cotton, wool and silk, including designs by one of Turkey's foremost fashion designers, Nesilihan Yargıcı.
H13 ✉ İstiklâl Caddesi 123–5, Beyoğlu ☎ 251 4092 🕐 Mon–Sat 9:30–6 🚇 Taksim

PATISSERIES AND SWEET SHOPS

BEBEK BADEM EZMESI
This wonderful establishment has been trading in almond and pistachio fondant since 1904.
✠ L9 ✉ Cevdet Paşa Caddesi 238/1, Bebek ☎ 263 5984 🕓 Mon–Sat 9:30–6

ÇIKOLATA EVI
An irresistible opportunity to pick 'n' mix your own top-quality chocolates.
✠ Off map at O19 ✉ Bağdat Caddesi 304, Caddebostan ☎ 346 6520 🕓 Mon–Sat 9:30–6

HACI BEKIR
The best possible introduction to Turkish delight.
✠ H13 ✉ İstiklâl Caddesi 129, Beyoğlu ☎ 245 1375 🕓 Mon–Sat 9:30–6 🚇 İstiklâl Caddesi

KOSKA HELVACISI
This long-established family concern is one of the best-known Turkish sweet shops in Istanbul. If you're not sure about any of the flavours, ask for a sample.
✠ L12 ✉ Yeniçeriler Caddesi 57 ☎ 517 0625 🕓 Mon–Sat 9:30–6 🚇 Çemberlitaş

PATISSERIE DIVAN
A chain of shops famous for its *marron glacé*, 'rococo' ice-cream cake and Black Forest gateaux.
✠ Off map at C16 ✉ Akçam Sokak 28, Levent ☎ 282 8492 🕓 Mon–Sat 9:30–6

PATISSERIE GAZEBO
Eat pastries to your heart's content in the luxurious surroundings of the Çırağan Palace, with super Bosphorus views.
✠ G16 ✉ Çırağan Palace Hotel Kempinski, Beşiktaş ☎ 258 3377 🕓 Mon–Sat 9:30–6 🚢 Beşiktaş Vapur İskelsi

PATISSERIE SUISSE
You may need your credit card here because the mouthwatering ice-creams, home-made truffles and chocolates don't come cheap but they are half price after 8:30PM!
✠ Off map at C16 ✉ Princess Hotel, Maslak ☎ 285 0900 🕓 Mon–Sat 9–9

PINOR
If you are waiting for the ferry back to Istanbul, stop for a cup of tea at this patisserie, which has a mouthwatering selection of *baklava*, *çikolata*, *kurabiye* and more.
✠ Off map at C19 ✉ Dereboyu Caddesi 17/1, Sarıyer ☎ 242 3849 🕓 Mon–Sat 9:30–6 🚢 Sarıyer

PUDDING SHOP
No longer as trendy as it was in the 1960s and 1970s, although it still produces a fine *fırın sütlaş* (baked rice pudding).
✠ L12 ✉ Divan Yolu 18, Sultanahmet 🕓 Mon–Sat 9:30–6 🚇 Sultanahmet

SARAY
Turks come here to breakfast on pastries, but the shop is also famous for its Turkish milk puddings.
✠ F14 ✉ Teşvikiye Caddesi 137/A, Nişantaşı ☎ 275 3948 🕓 Mon–Sat 9:30–6

Sweets
If you have a sweet tooth you will find Istanbul an earthly paradise. Turkish pastries have an extremely high sugar content and are also rich in butter, so forget the calorie counting! Among the most famous delicacies are, of course, Turkish delight (*lokum*) and *baklava*, a syrupy pastry filled with pistachios or walnuts. You might also like to try the puddings, made either from chocolate (*süpangle*) or rice (*sütlaş*).

JEWELLERY

Golden rule

Surprisingly, the Spice Bazaar (➤ 32) is also home to a number of reputable jewellers. Gold, especially, is a good buy in Turkey because, while the standard of workmanship is high, labour costs are much lower than in the rest of Europe or the United States. Make sure that any purchases are stamped and carry a label of warranty from the Turkish Standards Institute.

DIAMOND
Located in the large Galleria Shopping Mall off Kennedy Caddesi, this exclusive store has a wide range of jewellery and brand watches.
➕ Off map at O7 ✉ Galleria Shopping Mall, Ataköy Sahil Yolu ☎ 559 7634 🕐 Mon–Sat 9:30–6

FEYZAN
Most tourists come to the Spice Bazaar for tea and Turkish delight, but it is also home to a number of jewellery stores such as Feyzan.
➕ K12 ✉ Mısır Çarşısı 5, Eminönü ☎ 519 3641 🕐 Mon–Sat 9:30–6 🚇 Eminönü

GÜLBIN
The proprietors, Namık and Tahsin, will show you their impressive collection of gold rings, chains, earrings and necklaces in 14 to 22 carats.
➕ K12 ✉ Mısır Çarşısı 10, Eminönü ☎ 512 6243 🕐 Mon–Sat 9:30–6 🚇 Eminönü

KAPALI ÇARŞI (COVERED BAZAAR)
This famous market has more outlets specialising in jewellery than any other item. There is even a Jewellers' Street (Kuyumcular Caddesi).
➕ L12 ✉ Nuruosmaniye Sokak, Beyazıt 🕐 Mon–Sat 8:30–7 🚇 Çemberlitaş

MÜCEVHER JEWELLERY
This exclusive store specialises in custom-made jewellery, including gold rings, necklaces and cuff-links. Each design is unique.
➕ E14 ✉ Rumeli Caddesi, Villa İşhanı 4– 6, Nişantaşı ☎ 241 3461 🕐 Mon–Sat 9:30–6

SOLITAIRE
An established firm specialising in original designs using 18-carat gold and diamonds. Each piece is custom made.
➕ Off map at C16 ✉ Akmerkez Shopping Mall 226, Etiler ☎ 282 0453 🕐 Mon–Sat 9:30–6

TIFFANY AND CO COLLECTION
This is an opportunity to shop in the luxurious surroundings of the Çırağan Palace Kempinski Hotel, the sole Turkish distributor of the legendary American firm.
➕ G16 ✉ Çırağan Palace Hotel Kempinski Çırağan Caddesi 84, Beşiktaş ☎ 259 3749 🕐 Mon–Sat 9:30–6 🚇 Beşiktaş Vapur İskelesi

URART
One of the best places to come if you are looking for something special to act as a memento of Turkey. All the silver earrings, rings and bracelets are inspired by ancient Anatolian designs.
➕ F14 ✉ Abdi İpekçi Caddesi 18/1, Nişantaşı ☎ 246 7194 🕐 Mon–Sat 9:30–6

GLASS & CERAMICS

AMPHORA
This shop near the Blue Mosque sells high-quality handmade ceramics produced by the Altin Çini Factory in Kütahya.
✚ M13 ✉ Arasta Çarşısı 147, Sultanahmet ☎ 563 8246 ⚙ Mon–Sat 9:30–5:30

ARTRIUM
A useful place to shop for up-market souvenirs. There's everything here from antique glass and ceramics to miniatures, Turkish soap and henna.
✚ J12 ✉ Tünel Passage 5–7, Tünel ☎ 251 4302 ⚙ Daily 9AM–9PM ⌂ Tünel

ELITE
Most of the glassware here is imported, including German Meissen, Swedish Ørrefors and Czech Moser.
✚ E14 ✉ Şakayık Sokak 63/14, Nişantaşı ☎ 232 4319 ⚙ Mon–Sat 9:30–5:30

KAPALI ÇARŞI (COVERED BAZAAR)
You'll find an excellent range of ceramics at competitive prices along the lane known as Yağlıkçılar Sokak.
✚ L12 ✉ Nuruosmaniye Sokak, Beyazıt ⚙ Mon–Sat 8:30–7 ⌂ Çemberlitaş

PAŞABAHÇE
The leading glassware manufacturer in Turkey also owns a retail chain with branches throughout the city.
✚ J13 ✉ İstiklâl Caddesi 314, Beyoğlu ☎ 244 0544 ⚙ Mon–Sat 9:30–5:30 ⌂ Tünel.

✚ O17 ✉ Söğütlüçeşme Caddesi 29, Kadıköy ☎ 683 0231 ⚙ Mon–Sat 9:30–5:30 ⌂ Kadıköy

SADBERK HANIM MUSEUM SHOP
Before leaving the excellent museum itself (➤ 47), call in at its shop, which sells high-quality ceramics at commensurate prices.
✚ Off map at C19 ✉ Sadberk Hanım Müzesi (➤ 47) ☎ 242 3813 ⚙ Thu–Tue 10:30–5 ⌂ Sarıyer Vapur İskelesi

TOLGA & SONS
This outlet specialises in rare Ottoman ceramics, but also sells European paintings and chinaware.
✚ Off map at C16 ✉ Nispetiye Caddesi, Peker Sokak 9, Levent ☎ 282 8651 ⚙ Mon–Sat 9:30–5:30

TOPKAPI PALACE SHOP
Located in the First Courtyard of the palace, this souvenir shop sells a variety of glassware and ceramics.
✚ L13 ✉ Topkapı Sarayı (➤ 42) ☎ 512 0480 ⚙ Wed–Mon 9:30–5 ⌂ Gülhane

YILDIZ PORCELAIN FACTORY
Just beside the entrance to the red-brick factory, in the grounds of Yıldız Palace, is a small shop selling the famous home-produced porcelain.
✚ F17 ✉ Yıldız Parkı ☎ 227 2949 ⚙ Mon–Sat 9:30–5:30 ⌂ Beşiktaş Vapur İskelesi

Yıldız porcelain

Taking a lead from Sèvres and Dresden, Yıldız porcelain made its first appearance in 1895 in the grounds of Sultan Abdülhamid's palace (➤ 46). The sultan called in experts from France and Germany to advise the local craftsmen on production techniques. The finest collection of antique Yıldız porcelain is on show in the Topkapı Palace Museum (➤ 43).

CRAFTS & ANTIQUES

Antiques galore

Istanbul probably has more antique shops per square kilometre than any other European city. You can buy everything from Ottoman furniture and fabrics to picture frames, candlesticks, glassware, prints and old coins. There are at least 85 shops packed into the narrow streets of the Çukurcuma district alone. Alternatively, take the boat to the Sunday market on Ortaköy waterfront, where you will find local artists selling handicrafts and paintings.

ANTIKARNAS

You will find a wide range of Ottoman as well as Turkish and European antiques and curios on sale in this Beyoğlu store.
🕂 H13 ✉ Kuloğlu Mahallesi, Faik Paşa Yokuşu 15, Çukurcuma ☎ 251 5928 🕐 Mon–Sat 9:30–5:30

ANTIKHANE

The largest antique warehouse in Turkey has nine floors of Islamic and oriental arts, paintings, Ottoman furniture, prints, maps and books.
🕂 H13 ✉ Faik Paşa Yokuşu 41, Çukurcuma ☎ 251 9587 🕐 Mon–Sat 9:30–5:30

ISTANBUL HANDICRAFTS CENTRE

You can watch the craftsmen at work in this restored *medrese*, next door to the Yeşil Ev Hotel.
🕂 L13 ✉ Kabasakal Caddesi 3, Sultanahmet ☎ 517 6782 🕐 Mon–Sat 9:30–5:30 🚇 Sultanahmet

KAPALI ÇARŞI (COVERED BAZAAR)

Inside the 15th-century İç Bedesten, in the heart of the bazaar, you'll find dealers specialising in old coins, brass and copper items and even small arms.
🕂 L12 ✉ Nuruosmaniye Sokak, Beyazıt 🕐 Mon–Sat 8.30–7 🚇 Çemberlitaş

LEVANT KOLEKSIYON

This fascinating shop specialises in 19th-century postcards, prints, books and ephemera.

🕂 J12 ✉ Tünel Meydanı 8, Tünel ☎ 293 6333 🕐 Mon–Sat 9:30–5:30 🚇 Tünel

MECIDIYEKÖY ANTIKACILAR ÇARŞISI

The Antique Dealer's Centre is a whole series of shops specialising in ornate 19th-century Turkish antiques, including furniture and porcelain.
🕂 C14 ✉ Tomurcuk Sokak 1–7, Mecidiyeköy ☎ 275 3590 🕐 Mon–Sat 9:30–5:30

MUDO PERA

Not strictly speaking antiques, but if you cannot afford the real article you can buy replica Ottoman *objets d'art* here.
🕂 H12 ✉ İstiklâl Caddesi 401, Beyoğlu ☎ 251 8682 🕐 Mon–Sat 9:30–5:30 🚇 Tünel

ODA

Authentic Ottoman antiques are on sale here, including plates, candlesticks, glassware and handmade wooden toys.
🕂 H13 ✉ Çukurcuma Caddesi 52, Çukurcuma ☎ 249 5051 🕐 Mon–Sat 9:30–5:30

SOFA ART AND ANTIQUES

This is a veritable treasure trove of old maps and prints, Kütahya pottery, calligraphy, silverware and other antiques.
🕂 L12 ✉ Nuruosmaniye Caddesi 42, Cağaloğlu ☎ 527 4142 🕐 Mon–Sat 9:30–5:30

BEST OF THE REST

ASADUR ZORIKOĞLU
This small shop specialises in excellent Turkish coffee.
➕ D18 ✉ Birinci Caddesi 94, Arnavutköy ☎ 263 5899 ⏰ Mon–Sat 9:30–6

BEŞIKTAŞ ÇARŞISI
This interesting food market, near Dolmabahçe Palace, sells fresh fish, fruit and vegetables.
➕ G16 ✉ Beşiktaş Caddesi, Beşiktaş ⏰ Mon–Sat 8–6 🚢 Beşiktaş Vapur İskelesi

GALATASARAY FISH MARKET (BALIKPAZARI)
A fish market, but much more besides. You will also find fresh cream, mushrooms, ducks, geese, quail, freshly baked bread, herbs and spices.
➕ H13 ✉ İstiklâl Caddesi, Beyoğlu ⏰ Mon–Sat 8–6 🚌 İstiklâl Caddesi

INTERNATIONAL BOOK HOUSE
One of the best places to come for English-language books, certainly if you are looking for best-sellers; also children's publications and cassettes.
➕ Off map at C16 ✉ Nispetiye Caddesi, Dr İhsan Aksoy Sokak 7/1, Etiler ☎ 257 9129 ⏰ Mon–Sat 9:30–6

KONYALI
This traditional Istanbul *charcuterie* sells the usual range of cheeses, cured meats, sausages, ready-to-eat *mezes*, salads and sandwiches.
➕ Off map at C16

✉ Emlak Kredi Çarşısı, Levent ☎ 268 2654 ⏰ Mon–Sat 9:30–6

MEGAVIZYON MUSIC & MULTIMEDIA
A large music store which sells everything from the latest cassettes and CDs to music literature, computers and computer software.
➕ H13 ✉ İstiklâl Caddesi 79–81, Beyoğlu ☎ 293 0759 ⏰ Daily 9:30AM–10PM ✉ İstiklâl Caddesi

MUZIK MERKEZI SANAT GALERISI
This shop near Gülhane Park specialises in Turkish and Asian musical instruments such as the *saz*, the *davul* and the *ney* (see panel).
➕ L13 ✉ Alemdar Caddesi, Sultanahmet ☎ 526 9031 ⏰ Mon–Sat 9:30–6 🚌 Gülhane

ROBINSON CRUSOE
A huge bookshop on two floors selling publications in a variety of European languages.
➕ H13 ✉ İstiklâl Caddesi 389, Beyoğlu ☎ 293 6968 ⏰ Mon–Sat 9:30–6 ✉ İstiklâl Caddesi

YENI KARAMÜRSEL (YKM)
Istanbul's largest department store has all the famous international and local brand names and designer labels. There's a cafeteria on the top floor and a supermarket in the basement.
➕ E14 ✉ Halaskârgazi Caddesi 368, Şişli ☎ 248 4120 ⏰ Mon–Sat 9:30–6

Music shops
Lovers of traditional Turkish music, inspired perhaps by the musicians who perform nightly in the Çiçek Pasajı, make a beeline for Galip Dede Caddesi, a street near the Galata Tower full of shops selling authentic instruments. You can choose from the *saz* (a kind of mandolin, dating back to the 12th century), the *ney* (a flute favoured by the Dervishes) or the *davul* (drum), which originated in the Janissary regimental bands.

Arts Venues & Cinemas

Films

Movies are very popular in Istanbul and you will find cinemas all over town, especially on İstiklâl Caddesi, around Şişli and on Bahariye Caddesi in Kadiköy on the Asian side. All films are shown with Turkish subtitles (including the latest American releases). Prices are very reasonable and matinées cheaper still. If you are here in April, look out for the annual Istanbul Film Festival, when contemporary Turkish and foreign films are screened at venues all round the city, including the Atatürk Cultural Center (see main text). Turkish films are shown with English subtitles.

AKSANAT CULTURAL CENTRE

A popular venue for programmes of classical music, jazz concerts and films shown on large laser–disc screen. Also painting and sculpture exhibitions and theatre performances.

H13 ⊠ İstiklâl Caddesi, Akbank Building, Beyoğlu ☎ 252 3500
🕐 Performances usually start at noon and 5:30PM
🚇 İstiklâl Caddesi

ALKAZAR CINEMA CENTRE

H13 ⊠ İstiklâl Caddesi 179, Beyoğlu ☎ 245 7538 🕐 See the *Turkish Daily News* for programmes and times
🚇 İstiklâl Caddesi

ATATÜRK CULTURAL CENTER (AKM)

This is far and away the largest and most important entertainment complex in Istanbul. For information on current productions, call in at the booking office at the front of the theatre; tourist information offices also have performance schedules. AKM is also a major venue of the annual Istanbul International Festival, which takes place in June and July (☎ 293 3133 or 251 1999). There are regular performances by the Istanbul Opera and Ballet Company, the Istanbul Symphony Orchestra and the Istanbul Theatre Company. Visiting companies from abroad, such as the St Petersburg Ballet Company, also perform at the AKM.

G13 ⊠ Taksim Meydanı ☎ 251 5600
🕐 Daily 9–9. Performances usually start at 7PM 🚇 Taksim

AYA IRINI

This beautiful 6th-century church is open for concerts during the annual Istanbul International Festival (June and July). Also ► 50.

L13 ⊠ First Courtyard, Topkapı Sarayı ☎ 293 3133 (festival)
🕐 Only for concerts
🚇 Gülhane

CEMAL REŞİT REY CONCERT HALL

An attractive concert hall generally used for chamber orchestra performances and recitals, as well as art exhibitions.

F14 ⊠ Harbiye ☎ 240 5012
🕐 Performances usually start at 7:30PM

FITAŞ

A large cinema with five screens.

H13 ⊠ İstiklâl Caddesi, Fitaş Pasajı 24–6, Beyoğlu ☎ 249 0166
🕐 See the *Turkish Daily News* for programmes and times 🚇 İstiklâl Caddesi

SULTANAHMET CAMII

The 17th-century Blue Mosque is the backdrop each evening from June to September to a dramatic *son et lumière* relating the history of Istanbul.

M13 ⊠ Sultanahmet Meydanı, Sultanahmet
🕐 Performances start at 9PM 🚇 Sultanahmet

TURKISH BATHS

BATHS OF ROXELANA

Located between the
Sultanahmet Camii and
Ayasofya, this double-
domed bath-house, now a
carpet salesroom, was
built by Mimar Sinan in
1556 and stands on the
site of the great Byzantine
baths of Zeuxippus.
Although the restoration is
less than ideal, you can
still see the coloured glass
and fountain in the
entrance hall (*camekan*)
and the fine marbles in
what was once the hot
room (*hararet*).
➕ L13 ✉ Sultanahmet
Meydanı 🕐 Mon–Sat
10–5 🚇 Sultanahmet

CAĞALOĞLU BATHS

Founded more than 250
years ago in the reign of
Mahmut I, these double
baths (men and women)
are probably the most
famous in Istanbul. The
dome-vaulted steam room
(*hararet*) is particularly
impressive.
➕ L12 ✉ Professor
Kazım İsmail Gürkan
Caddesi, Sultanahmet
☎ 522 2424 🕐 Men:
daily 7AM–10PM. Women:
daily 8AM–8PM

ÇEMBERLİTAŞ BATHS

The widow of Selim II,
Valide Sultan Nur Banu,
founded these splendid
baths in 1583. Although
the women's section was
pulled down in the 19th
century, the baths are still
divided into the traditional
male and female sections.
The masseurs are friendly
and happy to initiate first-
timers into bath rituals.
➕ L12 ✉ Vezirhanı
Caddesi 8, Divan Yolu,
Çemberlitaş ☎ 522 7974
🕐 Daily 6AM–midnight
🚇 Çemberlitaş

GALATASARAY BATHS

There has been a bath-
house on this site since
the reign of Bayezid II in
the early 16th century.
Standing next to
Galatasaray High School,
which used to own the
baths, their central
location makes them
popular with tourists.
➕ H13 ✉ İstiklâl
Caddesi, Beyoğlu ☎ 249
4342 🕐 Daily 8–8
🚇 İstiklâl Caddesi

GEDİK PAŞA BATHS

Dating from 1475, these
magnificent baths, recently
restored, may well be the
oldest in the city. The
founder, Gedik Ahmet
Paşa, was grand vizier
under Mehmet the
Conqueror and commander
of the Ottoman fleet. The
hammam is capped by an
impressive dome and
flanked by alcoves and
cubicles faced with marble.
A popular meeting place
for locals, these baths are
spacious, with 27 basins in
the men's section and 21 in
the women's.
➕ L12 ✉ Gedik Paşa
Caddesi 🕐 Daily 8–8
🚇 Çemberlitaş

TAHTA MİNARE BATHS

Located in the former
Jewish neighbourhood of
Balat on the shores of the
Golden Horn, these baths
are one of the city's oldest.
➕ H10 ✉ Yıldırım
Caddesi, Balat 🕐 Daily
8–8

Bath etiquette

First, undress and lock
your clothes in the cabin
provided. Someone will
give you a towel to wrap
around your body and
slippers for your feet. You
will then be shown to the
hot room, where you will
sweat it out for 15 minutes
lying on a warm marble
slab. The 15-minute
massage which follows
is optional (but
recommended). The
attendant will then lead
you to the washroom for a
good soap-down before
showing you to your
cabin, where you should
take another 15-minute
rest before leaving. Take
plenty of change as it is
customary to tip each of
your attendants.

CABARETS & NIGHTCLUBS

Summer nights

It is becoming common practice for nightclubs in Istanbul to open second venues in the summer. Most of them move out to seaside locations on the Bosphorus – Çubuklu on the Asian shore and Yeniköy on the European side, for example. There is a great outdoor atmosphere as the local crowd converges on the waterfront, dancing, promenading or sipping cocktails beneath beach umbrellas while listening to the music.

ALEM
Top Turkish singers and dancers perform in this popular out-of-town club.
🚹 Off map at C19
✉ Köybaşı Caddesi 10, Yeniköy ☎ 223 0012

CLUB 29
Disco music is the staple here, drawing a mixed, lively crowd. In summer the club looks out onto the water, and you wine and dine at tables shaded by umbrellas and lit by flaming torches.
🚹 Off map at C16
✉ Winter: Nispetiye Caddesi 29, Etiler.
Summer: Çubuklu
☎ Winter: 263 5411.
Summer: (216) 322 3888

ESKI YEŞIL
Popular with the acting community; the entertainment is old-time cabaret, Turkish style.
🚹 G13 ✉ Abdülhakhamıt Caddesi 61, Taksim
☎ 255 2020

GALATA TOWER NIGHTCLUB
Situated on the eighth floor of one of Istanbul's most famous landmarks. There are great views of the city by night as you watch the belly-dancing show or hit the disco.
🚹 J12 ✉ Kuledibi, Tünel ☎ 245 1160
🚇 Tünel

GAR MÜZIKHOL
'Music hall' here means glitzy showgirls, Anatolian folk-dancing and belly-dancing in a club near Yenikapı railway station.
🚹 M10 ✉ Mustafa

Kemal Paşa Caddesi 3, Yenikapı ☎ 588 4045
🚇 Yenikapı

KERVANSARAY
Expensive and showy. The club is renowned for the quality of its floor show, which includes folk- and belly-dancers.
🚹 G13 ✉ Cumhuriyet Caddesi 30, Harbiye
☎ 247 1630

ORIENT HOUSE
A spirited costume and belly-dancing show; drinks are on the expensive side.
🚹 L11 ✉ Tiyatro Caddesi 27, Beyazıt
☎ 517 6163 🚇 Beyazıt

PASHA
A large, trendy entertainment complex beside the Bosphorus, offering disco dancing as well as restaurants and bars. Summer only.
🚹 F17 ✉ Muallim Nacı Caddesi 142, Ortaköy
☎ 259 7061

ŞAMDAN ETILER
Very up-market, this busy club has a popular disco as well as a restaurant and bar. Reservations essential at weekends.
🚹 Off map at C16
✉ Nispetiye Caddesi, Etiler ☎ 263 4898

TAXIM NIGHT PARK
There is a disco, bar and restaurant in this club celebrated for its transvestite floor show.
🚹 G13 ✉ Feridiye Mahallesi Nizamiye Caddesi 12/16
☎ 256 4431

ROCK & JAZZ CLUBS

CAPTAIN HOOK
A newcomer to the music scene, Captain Hook presents live rock each evening from Wednesday to Saturday.
✚ G13 ✉ Cumhuriyet Caddesi, Kaya Apt 349/1, Harbiye ☎ 240 6849

EYLÜL
Live rock and jazz bands perform at this popular night spot just outside Ortaköy.
✚ C19 ✉ Birinci Caddesi 23, Arnavutköy ☎ 257 1109

GRAMAFON BAR
Live music nightly (except for Sundays) and a sophisticated ambience in this centrally located bar.
✚ J12 ✉ Tünel Meydanı 3, Tünel ☎ 293 0786
🚇 Tünel

HARRY'S JAZZ BAR
Live blues, rock, karaoke, cocktails and video shows are all on offer at this leading Istanbul hotel.
✚ G13 ✉ Hyatt Regency Hotel, Taşkışla, Taksim ☎ 225 7000

HAYAL KAHVESI
Rock, blues and jazz are on offer at this very popular music club; it has a summer branch on the waterfront in Çubuklu, Burunbahçe.
✚ H13 ✉ İstiklâl Caddesi, Büyükparmakkapı Sokak 19, Beyoğlu ☎ 244 2558
🚇 İstiklâl Caddesi

KEHRIBAR
Top-class music in this popular night spot close to Taksim.

✚ G14 ✉ Divan Oteli, Cumhuriyet Caddesi, Elmadağ ☎ 231 4100

MANDALA BAR
Live rock music is served up nightly by a variety of groups in this downtown bar.
✚ G13 ✉ Sıraselviler Caddesi 69/2, Taksim ☎ 293 6799

MEMO'S BIS
Come here for early evening drinks as you look out over the Bosphorus and listen to jazz and Latin sounds before dancing the night away. Happy hour 7–9PM.
✚ F17 ✉ Muallim Nacı Caddesi, Salhane Sokak, Ortaköy ☎ 260 8491

Q CLUB
The city's leading jazz club with quality international and Turkish acts. In summer the club moves out onto pier 84.
✚ G16 ✉ Çırağan Palace Hotel Kempinski, Beşiktaş ☎ 236 2121

ROXY
A lively bar featuring foreign and Turkish rock bands as well as jazz and pop groups.
✚ H13 ✉ Arslan Yatağı Sokak, Taksim ☎ 249 4839

Hayal Kahvesi

Very popular with 20-somethings, Hayal Kahvesi also welcomes foreign visitors and it makes for a great night out. To be sure of getting a table, arrive early, especially if you want to eat – it's sandwiches only after 9PM. Music is disco for most of the evening but there are also live Turkish rock bands at weekends.

HOTEL BARS

Rakı

The national drink of Turkey, rakı, is distilled from sweet raisins and flavoured with anise. The word derives from the Arabic araki ('sweating'), a reference to the distilling process. Most Turks drink rakı mixed with ice and water, which turns it a milky colour – the reason why it is referred to colloquially as the 'lion's milk'. Rakı production became a state monopoly in the 1930s. The local variety, Yeni Rakı, is 45 per cent proof.

BABIALI WINE BAR
An attractive, glass-domed bar on Ordu Caddesi, serving Turkish and foreign wines, champagnes etc.
🔒 L11 ⊠ Hotel Merit Antique, Laleli ☎ 513 9300 🚇 Laleli

THE ENGLISH BAR
Inspired by the typical British pub, this bar serves a wide variety of whiskies and ales.
🔒 G14 ⊠ Ceylan Intercontinental Hotel, Taksim ☎ 231 2121

GIRNE BAR
Cosy, friendly bar with a good location in old Pera. Live music in the early evening.
🔒 H12 ⊠ Hotel Mercure, Tepebaşı ☎ 251 4646

KÜPEŞTE BAR
Overlooking the Ataköy Marina. Live music is served up most evenings and the menu changes.
🔒 Off map at O7 ⊠ Holiday Inn, Crowne Plaza, Ataköy ☎ 560 8100

NEMESIS ROOF BAR
A quiet, relaxing bar with commanding views over the Bosphorus and the Ortaköy Camii.
🔒 F17 ⊠ Hotel Princess, Ortaköy ☎ 227 6010

NOBLESSE
Open from breakfast time to the early hours of the morning, the Noblesse specialises in international cocktails and there's live entertainment by Turkish and foreign artists daily except Mondays.
🔒 Off map at O7 ⊠ Renaissance Polat Istanbul Hotel, Yeşilyurt ☎ 663 1700

ORIENT EXPRESS BAR
Relive the days when passengers arriving from the Orient Express would drop in here to enjoy the excellent wines; the *fin de siècle* décor adds to the experience. Incidentally, this is where Agatha Christie wrote her famous crime novel, *Murder on the Orient Express*.
🔒 H12 ⊠ Pera Palas Hotel, Tepebaşı ☎ 251 4560

PERA BAR
Known as the 'meeting point', the Pera is a handy watering-hole for visitors to Taksim.
🔒 G13 ⊠ Savoy Hotel, Sıraselviler Caddesi 29, Taksim ☎ 252 9326 🚇 İstiklâl Caddesi

TEPE LOUNGE
The bar is on the top floor of one of Istanbul's tallest buildings, so wonderful views of the city are guaranteed. Live music every evening.
🔒 H13 ⊠ Marmara Istanbul Hotel, Taksim ☎ 251 4696 🚇 Taksim

VIEW BAR
The name says it all! The views from the bar are of the Sea of Marmara and they are unmatchable. Live music nightly between 6 and 8PM.
🔒 Off map at O7 ⊠ Çınar Hotel, Yeşilköy ☎ 663 2900

OTHER BARS

ABDÜLCABBAR CAFÉ BAR
Neco the barman mixes 101 cocktails as you listen to the live vocals in a bar which claims to be more than 600 years old.
H13 ⊠ Mis Sokak 11, Beyoğlu ☎ 243 6395
🚇 İstiklâl Caddesi

ANDROMEDA
Popular with the young set, Andromeda stays open until 3AM. It's noisy with pounding disco music.
G13 ⊠ Elmadağ Caddesi 11, Taksim
☎ 247 4538

BEBEK
An ideal place to relax, this quiet bar is in an attractive location overlooking the marina.
Off map at C19 ⊠ Cevdet Paşa Caddesi 15, Bebek ☎ 263 3000

CAFÉ GUITAR
Popular with university students, attracted perhaps by its American-style rock bar atmosphere. The live music three nights a week is cheap at the price.
H13 ⊠ Ayhan Işik Sokak 11/1, Beyoğlu
☎ 251 9832 🚇 İstiklâl Caddesi

ESCOBAR
Head 'south of the border' for an evening with authentic Mexican cooking, beers, tequilas and a boisterous atmosphere.
Off map at C16 ⊠ Çalıkuşu Sokak 13, Levent ☎ 281 9149

FIFTIES
Return to America of the 1950s with jukeboxes, soda fountains, gas pumps and posters of James Dean.
Off map at C16 ⊠ Nispetiye Caddesi 24, Etiler ☎ 283 5050

JASMINE CAFÉ BAR
One of the best places to go if you are a fan of traditional Turkish folk music. You're encouraged to join in and the musicians will hand you a *saz* (lute) if you want to improvise. There are hors-d'oeuvres on the menu as well.
H13 ⊠ Akarsu Sokak 10, Galatasaray
☎ 252 7266

KIRMIZI BAR
The 'Red Bar' is a newcomer to the Istanbul scene. As well as a terrace offering fabulous views across the Bosphorus, there is live music every night except Sundays and a menu offering Turkish specialities.
D18 ⊠ Kuruçeşme Caddesi 90, Kuruçeşme
☎ 287 2154

SULTAN PUB
A very lively bar in the heart of the old town, serving a variety of cocktails and, if you wish, French and seafood dishes.
L13 ⊠ Divan Yolu Caddesi 2, Sultanahmet
☎ 526 6347
🚇 Sultanahmet

YAGA BAR
The young-at-heart crowd here is drawn mainly by the music – live reggae and blues.
H13 ⊠ Zambak Sokak 6, Beyoğlu ☎ 244 5710
🚇 İstiklâl Caddesi

Bar scene
Istanbul's bar scene is pretty similar to that in all cities around the world. If you want a drink with a view, head for one of the downtown hotels or take a taxi to Ortaköy or another waterfront location. If you haven't anywhere specific in mind, Taksim probably has the greatest concentration of bars and plenty of variety. Avoid the backstreets and especially *gazinos* (sleazy bars with Turkish floor shows and hostesses) where foreigners are regularly ripped off, robbed and even assaulted.

83

LUXURY HOTELS

Pera Palas

Istanbul's most celebrated hotel, the Pera Palas, opened in 1895 specifically to cater for passengers arriving in Constantinople after their 68-hour journey on the Orient Express. The last word in luxury, the hotel acquired its aura of mystery and suspense after Agatha Christie stayed here while writing her novel *Murder on the Orient Express*. Other famous guests over the years have included the spy Mata Hari, the actress Sarah Bernhardt and the film star Greta Garbo.

ÇIRAĞAN PALACE HOTEL KEMPINSKI

Recently voted one of the top 100 hotels in the world, the Çiragan is a 19th-century sultan's palace with magnificent views across the Bosphorus and every conceivable luxury.
➕ G16 ✉ Çiragan Caddesi 84, Beşiktaş ☎ 258 3377 🚢 Beşiktaş Vapur İskelesi

DIVAN

This refurbished hotel has one of the finest restaurants in Istanbul, also called the Divan.
➕ G13 ✉ Cumhuriyet Caddesi 2, Taksim ☎ 231 4100

FOUR SEASONS

A Turkish prison dating from 1919, although there is nothing penal about the facilities here. The location, between Ayasofya and the Blue Mosque, is perfect for old town sightseeing.
➕ M13 ✉ Tevkifhane Sokak 1, Sultanahmet ☎ 638 8200 🚇 Sultanahmet

HOTEL MERIT ANTIQUE

Dating from the turn of the century, this hotel has been fully modernised and facilities include several restaurants and a health club. Attractively situated only 100m from the Covered Bazaar.
➕ L11 ✉ Ordu Caddesi 226, Laleli ☎ 513 9300 🚇 Laleli

KALYON

Located on the coast road; the sea views are the principal attraction of this modern hotel.
➕ M13 ✉ Sarayburnu, Sahil Yolu ☎ 517 4400

PERA PALAS

All rooms are beautifully renovated but simply furnished. Views of the Golden Horn. (See also panel.)
➕ H12 ✉ Meşrutiyet Caddesi 98–100, Tepebaşı ☎ 251 4560

PRESIDENT

A modern hotel in the heart of the old town. Facilities include an indoor swimming pool and sun-deck.
➕ L12 ✉ Tiyatro Caddesi 25, Beyazıt ☎ 516 6980

SWISSÔTEL THE BOSPHORUS

This is a vast modern complex with more than 600 rooms, 74 long-stay apartments, nine restaurants, outdoor and indoor swimming pools, gym, sauna and even tennis-courts. The views from the hilltop setting are spectacular.
➕ G15 ✉ Balyıldım Caddesi, Maçka ☎ 259 0101

YEŞİL EV

Wonderfully located behind the Blue Mosque, the rooms in this small, well-known hotel have period decor. The garden restaurant is recommended.
➕ M13 ✉ Kabasakal Caddesi 5, Sultanahmet ☎ 517 6785

SPECIAL LICENCE HOTELS

ALZER
A popular hotel in a good location near the Blue Mosque. Expect an early morning call to prayer, courtesy of the local muezzin.
➕ M13 ✉ At Meydanı 72, Sultanahmet
☎ 516 6262

AYASOFYA
Just a few minutes' walk from the Blue Mosque and other attractions, this small hotel has recently been rebuilt in the traditional Ottoman style.
➕ M12
✉ Küçükayasofya, Demirci Reşit Sokak 28, Sultanahmet ☎ 516 9446

AYASOFYA PENSIONS
A row of beautifully converted historic wooden Ottoman houses almost next door to Topkapı Palace. Neighbourhood restaurants.
➕ M13 ✉ Soğukçeşme Sokak, Sultanahmet
☎ 513 3660

DILSON
This modern hotel in the busy Taksim district is handy for shopping and nightlife. All rooms have air-conditioning and satellite TV.
➕ G13 ✉ Sıraselviler Caddesi 49, Taksim
☎ 252 9600

ELAN
Recently renovated, this small hotel is located in the main shopping area and has fine views of the Golden Horn.
➕ H12 ✉ Meşrutiyet Caddesi 213, Tepebaşı
☎ 252 5449

KARIYE
A beautifully restored hotel in an historic wooden mansion, next door to the famous Kariye Camii. Garden, restaurant and bar.
➕ H9 ✉ Kariye Camii Sokak 18, Edirnekapı
☎ 534 8414

OTEL OBELISK
An attractively converted 19th-century wooden Ottoman house with a terrace restaurant overlooking the Sea of Marmara. Well located for sightseeing.
➕ M12 ✉ Amiral Tafdil Sokak 17–19, Sultanahmet
☎ 517 7173

PIERRE LOTI
This small, attractive hotel in the heart of the old town takes its name from the 19th-century French novelist who fell in love with Istanbul and made his home here.
➕ L12 ✉ Piyerloti Caddesi 5, Çemberlitaş
☎ 518 5700

SARI KONAK
A small, beautifully furnished, modern hotel with a rooftop garden overlooking the Sea of Marmara.
➕ M13 ✉ Mimar Mehmet Ağa Caddesi 42–6, Sultanahmet
☎ 638 6258

VARDAR PALACE HOTEL
Close to Taksim Square, this restored hotel opened in 1990 in a building that is 100 years old.
➕ G13 ✉ Sıraselviler Caddesi 54–6, Taksim
☎ 252 2896

Special licence hotels
'Special licence' hotels are converted listed buildings of historic or architectural importance. Typical are the brightly painted wooden houses of the Sultanahmet district, such as the Ayasofya Pensions (see main text). Bear in mind that this unique accommodation is in great demand, so you should book well in advance. If you want to stay in one of these hotels, write for further information to the Turkish Touring and Automobile Club (✉ Soğukçeşme Sokak, Sultanahmet ☎ 513 3660).

BUDGET ACCOMMODATION

Room with a view

If you're a budget traveller and can't afford to stay in a first-class hotel, you should at least be able to find a 'room with a view'. Even lower-priced hotels often have a rooftop breakfast room or terrace bar. If the idea appeals to you, try for accommodation in Taksim, which overlooks the Bosphorus; Sultanahmet, for views of the Sea of Mamara; or in Beyoğlu (the Golden Horn).

BEBEK

A small, no-frills hotel in one of the loveliest districts of Istanbul, about 10km from the city centre. Only the rear rooms have Bosphorus views.

➕ Off map at C19
✉ Cevdet Paşa Caddesi 113–115, Bebek ☎ 263 3000

BÜYÜK LONDRA

Many rooms in this delightful old building – decorated in traditional Ottoman style – have balconies overlooking the Golden Horn. Excellent value.

➕ H12 ✉ Meşrutiyet Caddesi 117, Tepebaşı
☎ 293 1619

CORDIAL HOUSE

A clean, comfortable hotel with basic amenities, situated just off the ancient Roman road, Divan Yolu Caddesi, in the heart of the city's old town.

➕ L12 ✉ Peykhane Sokak 29, Çemberlitaş
☎ 518 0575

GRAND LORD

All rooms in this comfortable, budget hotel in a popular area of Istanbul have TV and private shower. Friendly, helpful staff.

➕ L11 ✉ Azımkar Sokak 22–4, Laleli ☎ 518 6311

ANTIQUE

Budget accommodation in a residential area not far from the Hippodrome and other old town sights. Terrace bar.

➕ M12 ✉ Oğul Sokak

17, Sultanahmet
☎ 516 4936

HIPPODROME

This former Ottoman house has a good central location close to the Blue Mosque.

➕ M13 ✉ Mimar Mehmet ağa Caddesi 17, Sultanahmet ☎ 517 6869

PARK

All rooms in this comfortable, centrally located hotel have a private shower. The roof terrace overlooking the Sea of Marmara is a real bonus.

➕ M13 ✉ Utangaç Sokak 26, Sultanahmet
☎ 517 6596

STAR

A budget hotel with 26 rooms, right in the heart of things just off Taksim Square.

➕ G13 ✉ Sağlık Sokak 11–13, Gümüşsuyu
☎ 293 1860

TAYHAN

A modern hotel in the quaintly dilapidated Kumkapı district, ideally situated for the neighbourhood fish restaurants. Two bars.

➕ M12 ✉ Kadırgalimanı Caddesi, Kumkapı
☎ 517 9525

TURKOMAN

The rooftop breakfast room in this historic building near the Hippodrome has some of the best views in the city. All rooms have TV.

➕ M12 ✉ Asmalı Çeşme Sokak 2, Sultanahmet
☎ 516 2956

ISTANBUL
travel facts

ARRIVING & DEPARTING

Before you go

- Check visa requirements with your travel agent or the embassy in your country. Visitors from the US, the UK and Ireland can buy a three-month visa (£10) on entry. If travelling by train or car, you will need transit visas for Romania and Bulgaria.
- There are no compulsory vaccination requirements for Turkey. Up-to-date tetanus, polio, typhoid and hepatitis A immunisation is recommended.

When to go

- The best time to see Istanbul is in the summer, when the warm, dry days and mild evenings are ideal for enjoying the Bosphorus.
- June and July are also the months of the Istanbul Festival of Arts and Culture.

Climate

- Summers (mid-June to mid-September): temperatures rise to 28°C in July and August; cool evening breezes.
- Winters (October to mid-March): temperatures drop to 2°C in February.
- Rainfall is relatively high, especially in winter.
- An average of eight days' snow.

Arriving by air

- Istanbul Atatürk International Airport in Yeşilköy (☎ 663 6460) handles international and domestic flights.
- Most international airlines fly to Istanbul.
- Turkish Airlines (THY): ✉ Taksim ☎ 252 1106 or ✉ Atatürk Airport ☎ 663 6300.
- The white Havaş buses provide a regular shuttle service to Aksaray

in the old city and Taksim Square every hour between 6AM and 11PM (half-hourly during the afternoon). Alternatively, take a taxi to the centre (24km).

Arriving by train

- The journey from London takes about three days. Inter-Rail Cards are valid in Turkey.
- There are two main railway stations in Istanbul, both with left-luggage facilities: Haydarpaşa (Asian routes) ☎ 336 0475; Sirkeci (European routes) ☎ 527 0050.

Arriving by bus or coach

- There are regular sevices from France, Austria, Germany, The Netherlands, Italy and Greece.
- Turkish coach companies also operate to and from other European cities: Bosfor Turizm ✉ Taksim ☎ 251 7000; Ulusoy Turizm ✉ Taksim ☎ 249 4373; Varan Turizm ✉ Taksim ☎ 251 7481.

Customs regulations

- Duty-free allowances are: 200 cigarettes, 50 cigars, 200g tobacco, 0.5l spirits, 0.5l wine. There is an additional allowance of 400 cigarettes, 100 cigars and 500g tobacco if you buy from a Turkish duty-free shop.
- Any valuable items should be registered on your passport on entry.
- Keep proofs of purchase for expensive items, such as carpets – you may be required to produce them before departure.
- Exporting antiquities is forbidden.
- You may bring any amount of foreign currency into Turkey, but exchange slips should be kept as you may be asked to show them when you leave. You may take the

equivalent of US$5000 in Turkish lira in or out of the country.

ESSENTIAL FACTS

Alcohol
- Although Turkey is a Muslim country and many Turks prefer not to drink alcohol, it is widely available in restaurants and bars.

Electricity
- 220 volts AC; two-pronged round-pin plugs.

Etiquette
- Turkish people are generally friendly, polite and modest – you will earn their respect if you behave in the same way.
- You should adhere to the dress code for visiting mosques – longer skirts and trousers not shorts, long-sleeved tops, and women should cover their heads.
- Remove your shoes when entering a mosque and when visiting a Turkish house or apartment.

Insurance
- In addition to the usual travel insurance, you are advised to take out cover for health care, including an emergency flight home.

Lone and women travellers
- Foreign women travellers may be subject to unwelcome advances from some men who make assumptions about their morals.
- Avoid backstreets late at night – taxis are available in abundance.

Money matters
- Local currency is the Turkish lira (TL). Notes come in denominations of 5 million, 1 million, 500,000, 250,000, 100,000 and 50,000TL, and coins in 25,000, 10,000, 5,000 and 2,500TL.

- Exchange offices offer better rates than banks and hotels.
- Because of daily fluctuations in the exchange rate, do not change more money than you need.
- Keep all receipts – you may be asked to present them as you leave the country.
- A more convenient way to obtain cash is by credit card. There are cashpoint machines in banks throughout the city.
- Major credit cards are also accepted in the more expensive hotels and restaurants, airline offices and large shops.
- Travellers' cheques in US dollars or Deutschmarks can be cashed at banks or post offices displaying the 'Kambiyo' sign.

National holidays
- 1 Jan – New Year's Day
- 23 Apr – National Sovereignty and Children's Day
- 19 May – Youth and Sports Day
- 30 Aug – Victory Day
- 29 Oct – Republic Day

Opening hours
- Shops: Mon–Sat 9:30–6/7. Closed public holidays and first day(s) of religious holidays.
- Government offices: Mon–Fri 9–12:30, 1:30–5. Closed public holidays and first day(s) of religious holidays.
- Banks: 9–12, 1:30–5. Closed public holidays and first day(s) of religious holidays.
- Museums: Tue–Sun 9:30–5 (Topkapı Palace Wed–Mon). Closed 1 Jan, 23 Apr, 19 May, 30 Aug, 29 Oct, Şeker Bayramı, Kurban Bayramı.

Places of worship
- Mosques: most belong to the Sunni sect. See Top 25 Sights and pages 50–1 for listings.

- Greek Orthodox Patriarchate:
  ✉ Sadrazam Ali Paşa Caddesi, Fener
  ☎ 521 2532.
- Roman Catholic: St Antoine
  ✉ İstiklâl Caddesi 325, Beyoğlu
  ☎ 244 0935.
- Protestant: German Church
  ✉ Beyoğlu ☎ 250 3040.
- Anglican: Christ Church
  ✉ Serdar Ekrem Sok 82 ☎ 251 5616.
- Synagogues: Neve Shalom
  ✉ Büyük Hendek Caddesi 61, Şişhane
  ☎ 293 8795; Askhenazi
  ✉ Yüksekkaldırım Caddesi, Karaköy
  ☎ 243 6909.

Religious holidays
- The holy month of Ramadan, when Muslims fast between sunrise and sunset, lasts for four weeks before Şeker Bayramı.
- Şeker Bayramı (three days, dates vary).
- Kurban Bayramı (four days, dates vary).

Student travellers
- The following organisations will help with youth accommodation, camping, discounts and assistance with visa formalities:
- International Youth Hostel Association Center (IYHF)
  ✉ Alemdar Caddesi 26, Sultanahmet, Istanbul ☎ 520 9594.
- Gençtur Turizm ve Seyahat Acentası ✉ Yerebatan Caddesi 15/3, Sultanahmet ☎ 520 5274/5.
- 7 Tur Turizm Ltd ✉ İnönü Caddesi 37/2 Gümüssuyu, Taksim ☎ 252 5921.

Time differences
- Eastern Standard Time is two hours ahead of GMT.
- Daylight Savings Time runs from the last Sunday in March to the last Sunday in September.

Toilets
- There are toilets throughout the city near mosques and in museums and cafés. It is customary to leave a small tip in the plate by the door.
- A few old-style toilets (two footholds and a hole in the ground) have survived in Istanbul.

Tourist offices
- Official guides can be booked through tourist information offices (see below).
- There are also plenty of unofficial guides willing to help. Agree a price before you embark on a trip.
- Head Office ✉ Meşrutiyet Caddesi 57, Galatasaray ☎ 243 3472, 243 2928.
- Branches: Sirkeci Train Station
  ✉ İstasyon Caddesi 24, Sirkeci
  ☎ 511 5888; Sultanahmet Meydanı
  ☎ 518 1802.

Visitors with disabilities
- Istanbul is not an easy city for disabled visitors to negotiate. The streets and pavements are generally crowded and very uneven, and none of the public transport has facilities for the disabled.
- Some hotels have wheelchair ramps and most of the mosques and churches, as well as Topkapı Palace, are accessible to wheelchairs.

Where to get maps
- Bookshops in Taksim Square, İstiklâl Caddesi and the Covered Bazaar sell guidebooks, maps and dictionaries.

PUBLIC TRANSPORT

Taxis and *dolmuşes*
- The most common form of transport is the ubiquitous yellow taxi. Although more expensive than other means of transport, they are still relatively cheap and easily the most convenient way to get

around. All fares are metered. Higher rates apply after midnight.

- *Dolmuşes* (shared taxis) are even cheaper. They follow assigned routes and stop on demand. Destinations are indicated on the windscreen. Customers are charged according to the distance travelled.

Ferries

- Ferries ply up and down the Bosphorus and the Golden Horn.
- Timetables are posted outside the waiting room at each ferry dock.
- Buy a jetton from the ticket window and drop it into the turnstile. (Jettons are more expensive if you buy from the touts standing outside.) This will let you into the waiting area.
- When the boat is ready to leave, the doors will open for you to board. The main departure point is Eminönü, where there are six jetties (*iskele*) serving the Golden Horn, Bosphorus (round trip), Üsküdar, Kadiköy, Haydarpaşa (a car ferry) and Adalar (Princes' Islands). City Ferry Lines ☎ 244 4233.
- There is a 50 per cent discount on the Bosphorus round trip at weekends.
- There are also smaller private ferries which leave at frequent intervals. The destinations are called out and fares are collected on board.

Metro

- There are are only two short metro lines: the one-minute funicular ride between Tünel and Karaköy, and the new commuter line which begins at Yenikapı and connects Aksaray and Ulubatlı to the suburbs.
- Tickets are sold at the stations.

Buses and trams

- Bus routes are extensive, but travel is slow and the vehicles are crowded. There is a timetable and maps are on sale from main bus stations; maps are also displayed at many bus stops. A sign on the front of the bus indicates the terminus.
- Tickets (one per ride) must be bought at one of the terminals or from news kiosks which display the sign 'IETT bilet'. Drop the ticket into the box near the driver.
- There is also an electronic 'intelli-gent' multiple token on sale. Private buses (orange) take cash instead of tickets.
- There is a very limited tram service in Istanbul. Picturesque 19th-century trams run the length of İstiklâl Caddesi at irregular intervals.
- A new tram route extends from the quay at Eminönü into the suburbs and to the intercity bus terminal. For visitors, the most useful stops are Gülhane, Sultanahmet, Çemberlitaş, Laleli and the Topkapı Gate. Tickets are bought from the stand near the stop and put into the box at the entrance to the platform.

MEDIA & COMMUNICATIONS

Postal service

- Stamps are sold from post offices and from some shops selling postcards.
- Post boxes are yellow.
- It may be quicker and more reliable to leave your letters at a post office or hotel reception desk.

Post offices

- PTT (Post-Telephone-Telegram) signs are written in black on a yellow background.

- Main post office ✉ Yeni Postane Sokak, Sirkeci.
- The Sirkeci, Galatasaray Square and the Grand Bazaar offices are open Mon–Fri 8–8 (8–midnight for telephones and telegraphs); Sun 9–7.
- Other branches open Mon–Fri 9–12:30, 1:30–5.

Telephones

- You can make a call from any yellow or turquoise telephone booth using a phonecard (30, 60 or 100 units) or jettons (1, 5 or 10 units). Both are sold at post offices.
- International operator ☎ 115.
- Directory enquiries ☎ 118.
- The code for Istanbul is 212 (European side) or 216 (Asian side).
- For calls across the Bosphorus, dial 0, then the appropriate code.
- For international calls, dial 00, then, after the second tone, the country code and number.

Newspapers and magazines

- Newspaper kiosks sell a wide range of Turkish newspapers and magazines.
- There is an English-language paper, the *Turkish Daily News*, published Mon–Sat, which has national and international news.
- Kiosks at important tourist sights and the major hotels sell some international newspapers.

Radio and television

- The state-owned television network has five stations; satellite television is making inroads, causing fierce political debate.
- News bulletins in English and German are broadcast on TRT2 between approximately 10:30PM and 10:45PM following the Turkish news, and on TRT-INT at 9:15PM and 12:15AM.

- The larger hotels have satellite or cable TV receiving CNN, the BBC Prime Service, etc.
- There are also radio bulletins in English on TRT3 at 9AM, noon, 2PM, 5PM, 7PM and 10PM.

EMERGENCIES

Emergency phone numbers

You will need jettons to ring these numbers from public call boxes:
- Fire ☎ 110.
- Ambulance ☎ 112.
- Police ☎ 155.
- Tourism Police ☎ 527 4503.

Consulates

- Australia ✉ Tepecik Yolu 58, Etiler ☎ 257 7050.
- Canada ✉ Büyükdere Caddesi 107/3, Gayrettepe ☎ 272 5174.
- Ireland ✉ Cumhuriyet Caddesi 26 Harbiye ☎ 246 6025.
- UK ✉ Meşrutiyet Caddesi 34, Tepebaşı ☎ 252 6436.
- US ✉ Meşrutiyet Caddesi 104, Tepebaşı ☎ 251 3602.

Lost property

- Ask at your hotel desk or at a tourist information office (► 90).
- Lost passports should be reported to the Tourist Police ✉ Alemdar Caddesi 6, Sultanahmet ☎ 527 4503.

Medical treatment

- There is no free health care for visitors in Turkey. For minor ailments, go to a pharmacy. Many doctors in the main hospitals speak English.
- Private hospitals: American Hospital ✉ Güzelbahçe Sokak, Nişantaşı ☎ 231 4050; Florence Nightingale Hospital ✉ Abidei Hürriyet Caddesi 290, Çağlayan/ Şişli ☎ 224 4950; International Hospital ✉ Çınar Oteli Yanı, Istanbul Caddesi 82, Yeşilköy ☎ 663 3000.

- State hospital: Şişli Etfal Hospital (for emergency treatment) ✉ Etfal Sokak, Şişli ☎ 231 2209.
- Ambulance services: Gece (Night) Ambulance ☎ 247 0781; International Hospital Ambulance ☎ 663 3000; International SOS Assistance (Air Ambulance) ☎ 230 9638.
- Dentists: Cosmodent Dental Clinic ✉ Beytem Plaza, 4th floor, Şişli ☎ 296 1862 (English spoken).

Medicines

- Pharmacies sell imported drugs as well as local medicines.
- Pharmacists are qualified to take your blood pressure and administer first aid.
- Pharmacists operate a 24-hour rota service: addresses are displayed in their windows. Taksim Eczanesi ✉ İstiklâl Caddesi 16, Beyoğlu ☎ 244 3195; Altuğ ✉ Nispetiye Caddesi 40/3, Etiler ☎ 263 4079.

Sensible precautions

- Take sunglasses, a hat and high-factor sun-screen to protect yourself from the sun's rays.
- To prevent diarrhoea, avoid raw foods and ice cubes in drinks.
- Although tap water is officially safe to drink, it is heavily chlorinated. Bottled water is on sale everywhere.
- Keep a close eye on your valuables in crowded locations and don't leave them in hotel rooms.
- Mugging, bag-snatching and other street crimes are not common in Istanbul, but avoid isolated areas at night.
- Do not get into a taxi that already has a passenger.
- Use your judgement and generally act with the same caution as you would in other cities.

LANGUAGE

Pronunciation guide

c like j
ç like ch
ğ almost silent; serves to lengthen the preceding vowel
ı like i in sir
j like s in pleasure
ö like ur
ş like sh
ü like ew

Useful words and phrases

good morning günaydın
good afternoon iyi günler
good evening iyi akşamlar
good night iyi geceler
please lütfen
thank you teşekkür ederim
yes evet
no hayır
excuse me (in a crowd) pardon
do you speak English? ingilizce biliyor musunuz?
I don't understand anlamadım/ anlamıyorum
where is? ...nerededir?
what time? kaçta
how far? ne uzaklıktadır?
how much? ne kadar/kaça?
I want istiyorum

1 bir	7 yedi
2 iki	8 sekiz
3 üç	9 dokuz
4 dört	10 on
5 beş	100 yüz
6 altı	1,000 bin

Glossary

camii **mosque**
külliye **mosque complex**
medresa **religious college**
meydanı **square**
meyhane **tavern**
mihrab **mosque prayer niche**
mimbar **mosque pulpit**
müzesi **museum**
sarayı **palace**
türbe **mausoleum**

93

INDEX

CityPack
Istanbul

Written by   Christopher and Melanie Rice
Edited, designed and produced by
        AA Publishing

Maps   © The Automobile Association 1997
Fold-out map © RV Reise- und Verkehrsverlag Munich • Stuttgart
        © Cartography: GeoData

Distributed in the United Kingdom by AA Publishing, Norfolk House, Priestley Road,
Basingstoke, Hampshire, RG24 9NY.

The contents of this publication are believed correct at the time of printing. Nevertheless, the
publishers cannot be held responsible for any errors or omissions or for changes in the details
given in this guide or for the consequences of any reliance on the information provided by the
same. Assessments of attractions, hotels, restaurants and so forth are based upon the author's
own personal experience and, therefore, descriptions given in this guide necessarily contain an
element of subjective opinion which may not reflect the publishers' opinion or dictate a
reader's own experiences on another occasion.
We have tried to ensure accuracy in this guide, but things do change and we would be grateful
if readers would advise us of any inaccuracies they may encounter.

A CIP catalogue record for this book is available from the British Library.

ISBN 0 7495 1644 5

Published by AA Publishing (a trading name of Automobile Association Developments
Limited, whose registered office is Norfolk House, Priestley Road, Basingstoke, Hampshire
RG24 9NY. Registered number 1878835).

Colour separation by Daylight Colour Art Pte Ltd, Singapore
Printed and bound by Dai Nippon Printing Co (Hong Kong) Ltd.

Acknowledgements
The Automobile Association wishes to thank the following libraries and museums for their
assistance in the preparation of this book:
Robert Harding Picture library 31b; Kariye Museum 13a; Mary Evans Picture Library
12; Mosiac Museum 39; Sandberk Hanim Museum 47b; Spectrum Colour Library 20.
Clive Sawyer was commissioned to take the photographs for this book, with the
exception of the following which were taken from the Association's own Photo Library
with contributions from:
Paul Kenward 19, 41b; Dario Mitideri 37a, 49b, 54; Tony Souter 1, 5a, 18, 27a, 28, 41a,
43a, 49a, 59, 60, 63a, 63b.

Cover photographs
Main picture: Telegraph Colour Library Inset: Tony Souter

        Copy Editors *Hilary Hughes & Susi Bailey*
        Verifier *Mary Berkmen*
        Indexer *Marie Lorimer*

Titles in the CityPack series
•Amsterdam • Atlanta • Bangkok • Berlin • Chicago • Florence • Hong Kong •
• London • Los Angeles • Madrid • Montréal • Moscow • Munich • New York •
• Paris • Prague • Rome • San Francisco • Singapore • Sydney • Tokyo • Vienna •
• Venice • Washington, DC •